fall guy

Jeff King

Published by Silver Street Media
662 Silver Street
Agawam, MA 01001
Book Design by Kathryn Elias

Printed in the United States of America

Contents

Part Six

For Kathy

I wonder …

What would it be like …

To see Jesus face to face
To travel beyond the reaches of time
To find yourself at the center of heaven's timeless tale

What would it be like …

To bounce back after you bottom out
To get up after you've given up
To suddenly understand the purpose to your problems

I wonder …

Part One

Entry 1
A Storm at Sea

A flash of lightning explodes on the horizon, like the artillery of an approaching army.

"I don't like the looks of this," murmurs Peter.

I look up. A canopy of stars hangs overhead, shimmering in the night sky. Not a single cloud. Here on the open sea, far from the lights of the shoreline, the stars seem close enough to stretch out my hand and touch. I'm curious: Why would Peter feel anxious when, at least to me, the storm seems so distant?

We're in a simple wooden fishing boat. You know the type – maybe twenty feet long, a single sail on a sturdy wooden mast, a handful of old weathered oars. And we're crossing open waters. Our tiny boat slips along the surface of the sea, the water lapping against the wooden hull, the mainsail snapping softly in the breeze.

Minutes pass with barely a word being spoken. We're tired, tired from the events of the day. Even speaking seems an effort.

It is then that I feel the first real gust of wind, cold and unsettling. I look up into the sky. I see black clouds charging forward, galloping across the night sky, driving the stars from my sight.

Suddenly, without warning, the wind attacks, angry, tearing at our mainsail, driving us, tossing us. Lightning explodes and crashes around us. Thunder rolls across the water like cannon fire. Now cold rain pellets fall in an angry torrent, overloading my senses, leaving me gasping, sputtering, blinded. My clothes stick to my skin, weighing me down.

On the western horizon jagged mountains tower above the sea. Cool air, drawn down through the narrow passes, clashes with the hot, humid air hanging over the sea. Storms descend with an unbelievable fury as they roar down through deep gorges toward the open sea. Sudden, violent, unpredictable storms are common in this area.

Peter knows this. But I don't. I know only that, without warning, I have been pushed from a drowsy sunset cruise into a bone-jarring, breath-stealing battle.

I reach for the side of the boat, gripping its weathered wood, clinging with the desperate strength of a terrified man. The waves charge forward, pounding and slapping us, lifting and tossing us, pushing us farther and farther from the shore and deeper and deeper into the blackness.

We ride the curved spine of one particularly large wave, as it rears up, up, up, carrying us higher and higher. Then, as we reach the crest, we are momentarily airborne, flung free from its foaming grip. Our boat slams down with a bone-crushing crash. Immediately, with no time to recover, the next wave begins to lift us.

We watch one rogue wave, bigger still than the rest, rear steeply in front of us. We are unable to ride it. Slamming into it, the pointed bow of our boat is driven deep into its belly, thrusting like a knife plunged into the soft underside of an attacking animal.

Each wave now seems to be bigger than the last. Again and again our boat is plunged directly into the center of the rising wave. With each thrust, seawater cascades over our bow and we ride lower in the waves.

Through the howl of the wind, I hear Peter shout. "Get that sail down! We'll try to ride with the wind."

A moment later: "We're taking on water. Use those buckets to bail."

John, seated to my left, fumbles frantically, searching beneath the seat for something he can use to bail water. I see a wooden bucket behind my seat, but I'm too frightened to reach for it. I grip the side of the tossing hull with all my strength, as though the sheer intensity of my fear might be enough to hold the tiny boat above the waves. Yet I can see that no amount of bailing can hold back the fury of the sea.

In a white, searing bolt of light that splits the darkness, I see the faces of my friends: faces distorted with fear. Eyes wide. Hair matted. Chests heaving. Clothes clinging. We are moments from a black, violent, choking death.

In the jagged flash of light, I see terror.

Then I turn and look to the very back of the boat ... and I'm dumbstruck.

Jesus. Right there. Sleeping. He has pulled an old, faded cushion from beneath the coxswain's seat. Using it as a pillow, he has curled up in the back of the boat like an infant curled quietly in the womb.

Jesus. I see His face. He is content. I see his chest rise and fall slowly, deeply, with each breath. He is at peace. I have seen a toddler fall asleep, cuddled in his mother's arms, nestled soft against her heart, after a long summer's day of play. This is the look of Jesus, breathing deeply, resting in utter peace and security.

Peter reaches backward desperately to rouse Jesus. Shaking him roughly, he cries in a panic, "Don't you even care that we're about to drown?"

Jesus stirs. His eyes open. Has he been dreaming? (Of what world does Jesus dream when he dreams?) His eyes focus, adjusting to the dark. As he sits upright, an explosion of wind blasts back his hair.

We all begin shouting at once, one over the other. "We're done! This is it! Find something to cling to that floats!"

Peter pleads, "Lord, save us!"

Jesus stands. The boat leaps and kicks beneath him. He rides it like an untamed horse, pushing himself up from his seat, straightening both legs, raising one hand, then raising the other. In a raw explosion of light from a jagged spear of lightning, I see him. Robes billowing. Arms outstretched. Voice barely audible above the roar of the wind. So small in the center of the storm. He speaks.

"Quiet! Be still!"

Instantly – silence.

The storm is muzzled. The wind is out of breath. The flashing fury of the lightning passes. The ferocious whitecaps lie down, tired and spent. I watch the black clouds flee, now in full retreat, once again revealing a glittering, star-strewn sky.

At first, no one speaks. We look from one to another, locking eyes nervously, but not speaking a word. I hear the tired waves gently lapping the wooden hull of our tiny boat.

Jesus breaks the silence. "Why are you guys so afraid?" he says, his smile lighting up. He leans forward, draping his muscled arms over John and me. Then, with a grin, he gives us both a playful push. "Is your faith really that small?"

Not one of us dares to answer him. John simply turns to me and speaks in a quiet whisper, "Who is this, that even the wind and the waves obey him?" [1]

Who indeed.

Entry 2

Screams in the Night

The sky is still dark when we finally reach the opposite shore. I can't make out much of the landscape, but I hear the surf crashing, rolling up on a wide, sandy beach. Dunes and steep inclines are barely visible, making themselves known mainly by the opaque blackness that marks the delineation between the star-strewn sky and the great bulky mass of land.

Peter directs the boat toward the sounds of the beach. As the boat slices through the surf, James and John take hold of the lines, jump into the shallow water, and drag the boat to shore. Our bedraggled group climbs out of the boat, tired and stretching and glad to be on solid ground. I'm wet and cold and miserable. I can't stop shaking.

"Somebody gather some wood and get a fire going," directs Peter. "I've got some bread and cheese and a couple of fish that my mother-in-law, God bless her, sent along. We'll have some breakfast as we dry off."

"Got it," responds John. I join John, thinking the search for kindling will at least get my blood moving and help me shake off the cold.

John and I make our way into the darkness, climbing through the dunes into a meadow of tall grass. The foothills rise above us, great white limestone cliffs, pockmarked with caves and scarred with footpaths. As we hike upward, the sound of the surf grows distant. The chirping of crickets and katydids fills the night air, and the wind moves softly through the tall grass.

Suddenly, a horrible shriek pierces the stillness. John and I freeze.

"What was *that*?" I ask.

"Whatever it was, I think it was human," said John.

I'm not so sure. I'm thinking there's a mountain lion hunting up in the hills, or a bear, or some other kind of wild animal – and we're walking directly toward it. Whatever it is, it's not good; I know that much. I don't want to be anywhere close to it.

Just then, another shriek knifes through the darkness.

This time I'm certain: it's definitely human. I feel fear and dread surge through me like a current of electricity. The hair on the back of my neck is standing on edge and it's more than my cold, wet clothing that's making me shiver. I'm in a foreign country, in the dark, hiking up a lonely hillside – and violent, visceral screams fill the night. No, I don't want any part of this.

Just then two men come bursting out from the brush, running in our direction. Already on edge, I feel like I'm going to jump out of my skin.

"Stay back! Go! Run! It isn't safe!" they shout, breathless.

"But something's happening up there! Someone's being killed! It's happening right now!" argues John, motioning, pointing up into the hills in the direction the screams are coming from.

"The screaming – it's horrible! It sounds like someone is being tortured," I add.

They stop directly in front of us, blocking our path. "No one is being tortured," one says, shooting a nervous glance at the other. "At least … not in the way you are thinking."

He begins to tell us. "There is a man … if *man* is the word to describe him." He tries again: "There is one who is so tortured and tormented that …." His words falter.

"But, is he in danger? Is he alright?" I ask.

The man shakes his head. "No, he's *not* alright. Not at all. But there's nothing that can be done for him."

He explains that in the cliffs that rise above us there are old tombs that have been hewn into the limestone. In one of these old tombs, there lives a man whose very soul is twisted within him. He lives deep in the darkness, crawling about naked among the scattered bones, bits of clothing, and putrid decay. He drowns in a world of rage and violence and inhuman hatred.

"His ferocity is so great," continues the man, "that it is unsafe to be anywhere in this vicinity. At any moment, he may rush out with wild cries and horrible threats, springing upon anyone who might try to pass."

"But, surely…" John begins.

"We have tried tying him down," interrupts the other man. "In fact, we even tried chaining and shackling him. But he has a strength that is inhuman. He tears the chains to pieces!"

"But I heard him crying out," I say, unsatisfied. "I think he's hurt."

"No doubt he has done harm to *himself*," answers the man.

"He cuts himself with rocks. He throws himself into the stone walls of the tomb," offers the second man. "I work in this area – a herdsman – and I've seen him. It's terrifying! The sight of him! He wounds himself, slicing deep gashes into his arms and legs, his chest and face. Blood constantly covers his naked body."

I try to picture it, try to wrap my mind around what I am being told.

The other adds, "Day and night, he is constantly moaning and wailing, screaming and shrieking. He spits out curses and hatred with the intensity of a roaring fire that cannot be burned out. He strikes terror into any who come near."

I shift my feet uncomfortably, uneasy. I want to get out of here. "I think we need to get back to the others and let them know what's going on," I say.

John nods. "Jesus will know what to do," he says.

We turn and hastily make our way back down through the pre-dawn darkness, picking our way down the stony trail. The night is now eerily silent. The two herdsmen go with us. Jesus needs to hear this directly from their lips.

There is a sudden flutter of wings just behind us, as some birds are startled from their roost. *Are we being followed?*

I turn and see only shadows.

As we arrive on the beach, returning to our little group, I feel more secure. Someone has already found kindling and Peter has fish broiling over an open fire. The men huddle around it, seeking its warmth. John begins to introduce the two visitors.

Jesus stands and smiles brightly. He has a way of meeting people, lighting up as if he is once again connecting with an old friend he hasn't seen for a time.

I interrupt their greeting. "Sir, you need to hear this …"

But I never get a chance to finish my sentence …

From the shadows a man leaps into the firelight. He is naked, his face and chest glistening with fresh blood. Long, seeping gashes cover his arms and legs. Bruises mottle his limbs, old ones now the color of rust, fresh ones purple and blue. His hair is wild and matted, with clumps missing on each side. I smell the scent of death on him, the smell of open graves and old tombs.

The two herdsmen brace for the attack, knowing what is coming. The circle of men crouching around the fire leap up, startled and off-guard. We all back away quickly, trying to keep the fire between us and the intruder.

Jesus stands as still as a statue. He alone does not shrink back. Without speaking a word, he levels his eyes upon the hellish man, focusing with unblinking penetration. This man, whom chains and fetters could not hold, is now locked within the gaze of the one whom wind and waves obey.

Jesus draws in a deep breath. "Come out of this man!" he orders.

The creature shrieks in agony – the mindless, squirming, tortured torment of a man being burned alive, the wild-eyed scream of a man unable to bear a second more. He throws himself to the ground, his red-stained hands clutching the white sand of the beach, his fingers clenching in and out, in and out; his breathing labored.

In an inhuman voice, he screams, "What do you want with me, Jesus, Son of the Most High God?"

How can this insane man know anything about Jesus? I think.

Jesus locks his eyes upon the man, as a parent would lock his eyes upon a disobedient toddler in a test of wills.

The man kneels before Jesus, as a prisoner of war would kneel before a conquering king. "Swear to God that you won't torture me! I beg you!"

I am uneasy about what will follow. I toss a quick sidelong glance at John. He stands protectively in front of the herdsmen, who instinctively cower back beyond the circle of firelight.

The creature snarls, his shadow leaping and dancing, distorted in the jagged, jumping light of the fire. His body glistens with blood and sweat, his face is splashed with tears.

Quietly, Jesus asks, "What is your name?"

At the question, something in the man changes. I see it move across his face. His eyes look up, dead. His voice speaks up, alive – alive with the thousand-throated chant of a mob.

"My name is Legion … for we are many."

What could he mean? A Roman army legion?

All of a sudden, thoughts fly through my mind, rapid, one after another.

A legion consists of more than six-thousand men! Would he have us believe that all the forces of darkness have gathered in this one place, in this one man, to do battle with Jesus?

I think this poor man is insane – totally insane. But could there be more? Could this man be the home, the hive, of a swarming, stinging horde? Would evil intentionally position its strongest forces in the direct path of Heaven's Prince, choosing this as its battlefield?

If so, they have seriously misjudged. The battle seems lost before a single salvo can be fired. Legion grovels along the ground, writhing snake-like in the sand, begging and pleading.

He twists his face upward, arching his neck. "Son of God," Legion implores, "please do not send us into the Abyss. Not now. Not yet. Let us stay."

By now the sky is beginning to brighten. Pink fingers of light stretch over the hills; a faint, watery light spills over the landscape. I see the first glimmer of pallid light upon the sea. I can make out the dunes, the fields, and the pale limestone cliffs which tower over us. A short distance away, I see an enormous herd of pigs feeding on a nearby hillside, barely visible in the thin morning light.

Legion sees the pigs as well. They graze peacefully, a vast herd, two-thousand strong, stretching far across the rock-strewn hillside. Like a lizard eyeing an insect, Legion slowly twists his head toward Jesus. "Send us among the pigs," he begs. "If you drive us out, allow us to go into them."

Silence hangs in the air.

Seconds tick by.

"Go!" commands Jesus.

The instant the order is given, a wave of energy sweeps over the herd like a current of electricity. With heads jerking upward, and throats grunting and squealing a cacophony of cries, the entire herd races down the steep hillside in a frenzied rush. The creatures throw themselves into the sea. For one long minute, the water is white with their brutish splashing, kicking, choking. Then, stillness … and a silent sea littered with the brown corpses of the herd, bobbing in the gentle waves and washing up along the sandy shore.

And Legion ... or whoever he truly is now that the hive has been emptied of its angry swarm ... He-who-was-once-Legion takes a deep breath and looks about him as if seeing the world for the first time. He sits upright. He breathes in the clean, bracing air of the sea. He takes in the pale, silver light of the pre-dawn sky. Once more I see his face change before me. His eyes focus. His mouth, once fixed in a sneer, relaxes. He almost smiles. Whatever held this man's tortured mind is gone.

He is free.

Already one of our men has thrown a blanket over him. Another offers him a damp cloth to clean himself and a generous share of our food. The herdsmen, unsettled, disappear quickly, hurrying off in the direction of the little village, no doubt eager to report the remarkable events that led to the loss of their herd.

But He-who-was-once-Legion pays little attention to all of this. His focus is instead upon Jesus. He has experienced something with Jesus, something at a level that none of us yet understands. No doubt he tries to make sense of the drama that circled about him. He tries to make sense of the lost years.

He sits at the feet of Jesus, absorbing it all, soaking in the world with newborn senses. At last, he speaks. Gentle words. Emotional words. "Jesus, Lord ... please let me go with you when you leave. Please."

Jesus reaches out his hand, the two men clasp forearms, and Jesus pulls him up. They stand facing one another, arm clenching arm, eyes locked. With the tenderness of a father speaking to his son, Jesus answers with quiet authority: "No. You have been away from your family far too long ... it's time to go home."

Then, still clasping the man's arm, a smile begins to rise up upon Jesus' face, rising up as bright and beautiful as the Galilean sunrise. Laughing easily, he adds: "Go home to your friends and family and tell them how good God has been to you!"[2]

By now the sun has pushed completely above the white limestone cliffs, bathing the sea in sparkling light. There is only one thing that seems brighter ...

The smile of Jesus.

Entry 3
Twenty Minutes Earlier, Two-Thousand Years Later

The drama has passed. He-who-was-once-Legion has left us. Jesus and our little band of fishermen settle back to eat our meal.

Then it happens.

How would I describe it? A moment of light-headedness. The feeling of falling. The white-out … one second before you pass out.

There I am standing on the beach beside John, watching the fish broil on the fire and the gulls circle greedily overhead. A second later, without warning, I am falling. But here is the part that I can't explain: I topple not into the coarse, white sand of the beach …

I tumble into my office.

Let me say that to you again. I have the sensation of falling – for just a fraction of a second. In the next instant I am sitting in my office chair, staring at my computer screen.

I look at the clock. Twenty minutes have gone by since I last glanced at it.

And yet … and yet … two-thousand years have gone by.

I take a deep breath and let it out slowly. I look again at the clock beside my desk. Twenty minutes have slipped away unaccounted for. Yet I am certain … yes, quite certain … that I have spent the last fifteen hours in the grassy meadows and stormy seas of Galilee.

No, don't look to me for an explanation. I have none. I can't *explain* any of it – but I can *describe* it. So that's what I'll do. I'll write it down … get it out on paper … record it while it's still fresh. That's the only way I know how to deal with it. What you do with my story is up to you.

I swear only this: that every word I tell you is true.

I find a notebook in the closet, bring it to my desk, and open it. I stare at the empty pages.

God, what is happening to me?

My heart is pounding like a drum; my hands shake uncontrollably, the after effects of my surging adrenaline. I'm confused – and terrified.

What in the world just happened?

The obvious fact is staring me right in the face: I've had some sort of mental collapse, some sort of complete and utter break with reality.

Yet it felt so lifelike. Every moment I experienced over the past fifteen hours was so clear, so vivid – so real. I could feel the cold, stinging pellets of rain on my face. I could feel the coarse sand of the beach beneath my feet. I could carry on long, coherent conversations with others. Surely those fifteen hours could not be merely the hallucinations of a troubled mind.

I close my eyes tight, while intentionally slowing my breathing. I need things to look different when I open them again. I need to get a grip. I need to make sense of what happened.

Think, Jeff, I order myself. *Figure this out.*

I decide to search the internet for information. I google mental illness, insanity, psychosis, anything I can think of. Reams of information are available. But, the thing is: nothing matches my symptoms. I wasn't delusional, or paranoid, or schizophrenic – at least, I don't think I was. I wasn't hearing strange voices or spotting dark, sinister figures lurking in my peripheral vision. And no one was "reading my mind" or "controlling my thoughts" – classic signs of impaired mental health.

No, I was quite certain that I was in a complete, coherent world – just a *different* world, in a distinctly different time and culture. And, in this *different* world I was able to think logically, function appropriately in social situations, and maintain healthy relationships. Stranger still, I fit seamlessly into this world. I understood their language and customs; I enjoyed meaningful friendships; I looked and talked and dressed just as they did.

In short, I belonged.

Oddly, while immersed in this *different* world, I had no knowledge of what would happen next. Looking back on it, I would think that I should have known that Jesus would quiet the storm. After all, it's a beloved Bible story which I have known since childhood. It should have been obvious. But, believe me, that night, in the middle of the driving rain and pounding surf, I had no inkling that I would even survive the hour. The fear was real. The waves were real. The black sea, flashing lightning, and roaring wind were real. In my mind – and, apparently, in reality – the events had not yet unfolded. Our fate still hung in the balance. The miraculous events of that night were still years away from being recorded in the pages of Scripture.

No, this couldn't just be a hallucination! It was too real.

Suddenly, I think of another approach. I open my Bible and begin pouring through the details of the ancient stories within, reading with fresh eyes. Yes, yes, it all fits – even the details.

Every event, every word spoken, everything I experienced during those fifteen lost hours – it all matches up precisely with the ancient Biblical record.

I pull dusty books from my shelf that I haven't opened since my college years. I read of the customs and culture of First Century Galilee. I see a picture of a man dressed in exactly the type of clothing I saw the men wearing – and that I myself wore. I see a replica of a First Century fishing boat. Yes, it fits! Down to the smallest minutia! Down to the tiniest fragment of fact!

So, somehow, if I have hallucinated all of this, my mind somehow constructed a fully-formed, precisely-detailed world which fits exactly with historical fact. Yes, somehow my "delusion" is filled with abundant factual details which I did not even know prior to this. What do I make of this?

Just then it dawns on me: *It would take a greater leap of faith to believe that I was merely hallucinating than to believe that I was in reality, somehow, in some way, thrust into the First Century.*

Immediately a new fear leaps into my mind. Suppose this "fall" isn't just some weird thing that happened to me *one time only*. The idea sets off alarm bells. *Could this happen to me again?* I've been assuming this was just some strange experience that I lived through: I can't explain it, but … okay, it's over, in the past, deal with it. But what if this is more like some kind of reoccurring condition? Something that hits me like … let's say, a sudden seizure – a startling, debilitating loss of control that can strike at any moment, in any place, without any warning?

Oh, God, I can't live this way.

I'm afraid. Terrified. Filled with dread. Gripping the arms of my chair, staring at the pages in front of me, I think: *What if this happens to me all over again?* But my fears don't stop there: *And what if next time it lasts even longer?* Now my mind is racing. *What if I get stuck and can't return?*

I take a deep breath and slowly let it out.

What if I can't find my way back?

I breathe in deeply and clench the pen a little harder.

And I begin to write my story ….

I suppose I should back up, give you a little background. Okay, first … My name is Jeff … Jeff King. I'm a husband, a dad, and a grandpa. And I'm a pastor, a pastor who's been loving and serving the same church for more than twenty-five years. Go online. Check it out – it's all true.

And I am not crazy. At least, I don't think I am. I have no family history of mental illness. But, no, I have not talked to my doctor about this. And I have no intention of talking to my doctor – or anyone – about this. I mean, let's be honest, how would I begin such a conversation? "Sure, Doc, I feel fine. Thanks for asking. I just have a slight tendency to slip between millennia...." And, no, I am not seeing a therapist, I'm not on medication of any sort, and I'm not going through any type of midlife crisis. In short, I don't do drama. I'm not the type. I don't fit the bill.

So, that's me. But the truth is, this story is not about me. Not at all. Why would it be? Based on my own life, I have little to write. I'm average. Ordinary. But what I have witnessed is … extraordinary. That's why I will record my experience and let you judge for yourself.

Should I tell my wife about this "episode?" My children? I am sure if I shared this feeling, this experience, with the people I love I would only worry them. How could I place a burden on them when even I don't understand what I am going through?

On top of that, what if it costs me my job? I can picture my supervisors sadly shaking their heads, mumbling something about my "loss of credibility."

And so, I will share this only with you. I will document my experiences in detail, leaving a journal in the top left drawer of my desk at work, where I am sure it will be found if something happens to me ... or ...

If I can never get back.

One day, when it no longer matters how people view me, I can share what has happened to me in this way. One day these pages will answer some questions for my wife about the distant stare I can get in my eyes from time to time. One day my children will know what their old man has really experienced, where he has traveled, what he has learned. And they will understand ...

If I can never get back.

While those fifteen hours in Galilee are still fresh in my mind, I will quickly record a few impressions. The sights, the smells, the feel of the rain on my face and the beach beneath my feet are still vivid. But even more vivid are the discoveries I take away from those fifteen hours ... those fifteen hours, twenty minutes earlier, two-thousand year ago. I'm a pastor. I've read the Bible all my life. But, for fifteen hours ... fifteen *astonishing* hours ... everything I've ever read came *alive!* Perhaps some of the things I discovered will be helpful to you.

If you've ever felt like life has pulled the rug out from under you, like the storm clouds are gathering over you, this is for you …

The first thing you need to know is:

Jesus is more powerful than the storm.

Are you caught in a storm right now in your life? I think of Cindy. This week she called me with the news: "The cancer's back." After five years of being cancer free, the enemy is back, spreading its tendrils through her abdomen – and spreading its icy fingers through her life. "I'm just heartbroken because of what this means to my husband and children." Cindy is caught in the storm.

I think of Austin. Austin's oxycontin addiction has cost him his job, his friends, his dignity. He's stolen money from his parents and a credit card from his girlfriend's parents. He's maxed out their credit and their trust. Austin is feeling the storm winds.

And I think about myself. As storm clouds blow over the American economy, our ministry's future has grown darker and darker. There simply isn't enough money coming in to pay for the programs, the staff, the mortgage, my salary. Sure, losing your job isn't like losing your life. A weak spreadsheet is not comparable to cancer. But, when it's *your* problem, it feels pretty real. Yes, storm clouds are sweeping over me, too.

Maybe you feel the same. What's the storm in your life? Is it your marriage? Your money? Your health? Are you afraid you are going to go under? Do you have that sinking feeling? Let me repeat that first fact again. Read it slowly. Jesus is more powerful than the storm.

Whoever finds this and falls across these pages, learn well this truth. The wind may be against you. You may be going under. In fact, a legion of critics, complainers, or creditors may surround you and all the forces of evil may be aligned against you. But Jesus is more powerful. With a word, he can quiet the raging wind and crashing waves. With a word, he can send Legions fleeing. With just a word.

No matter how big your storm is, Jesus is bigger.

And the second fact is this:

You need to get in the boat.

When I look back on that confusing moment when I first "fell" into Galilee, stumbling headlong through millennia, slipping silently through centuries, I realize the most important decision I made was the decision I made at the very start of the adventure: I decided to get into the boat with Jesus.

I remember the moment. I was standing on the beach in Galilee. To my right was the sea; to my left, the city. Suddenly, Jesus called out to me, "Well, Jeff, are you coming? Jump in!"

At first, I was hesitant. Uncertain. Then, without a look back, I made my decision: I waded into the water, reached out my hand, and was pulled aboard. No, I didn't know where the journey would take me. But I got in the boat.

Maybe you've felt like that from time to time. Confused. Uncertain. Not knowing where the journey is going to take you. Perhaps you feel that way right now. I can tell you only this: the one critical decision I made was the decision to get into the boat with Jesus. That one decision changed the entire trajectory of what was to follow.

If you're staring at a sea of debt or a legion of troubles, you're probably wondering, "What do I do now? Where do I even start?" Start by getting in the boat. *Whatever your storm is, you don't want to be in the storm alone.* This one decision will change every other experience that follows.

Ask Jesus if you can ride with him. How? Picture Jesus being with you at this very moment. You don't need to be standing on the edge of the Sea of Galilee, looking into his eyes. Just picture him in the empty seat in your office or in the passenger seat of your car. Picture him standing before you with an arm on your shoulder or walking beside you as you lay out your entire situation to him. The fact is, he is with you always. Now ask him. Do it now. Ask him if you can stay with him the rest of the way. Don't even call it a prayer. Call it whatever you want. But from this point on, you're going his way. Even if storm clouds should gather, you're sailing with the one whom wind and waves obey.

The final thing I want to record while it is still fresh in my mind:

You're going to be alright.

Here is what struck me that night in the middle of the raging storm: A number of those men on that boat were expert sailors. Think of it! Peter and Andrew, James and John – they were professional fishermen. They knew all the ins and outs of handling a boat. They understood the proper angle of the sail and the optimum distribution of weight. They had certainly been caught in many a storm on that same sea over the years. Yet they turned to Jesus – Jesus who had never handled a boat, Jesus who had worked only as a carpenter with his father in Nazareth.

How could a former carpenter possibly help these expert sailors? How could they survive, when all their skill was not enough, and death in the furious waves was their certain fate? Completely at the end of their resources, completely at a loss, those frightened fishermen threw themselves upon Jesus as their only hope. They forgot that he had never sailed a boat; they forgot their own abilities; they thought only of the divine ability within him. And so they threw themselves utterly and completely into the all-powerful hands of Jesus.

This, too, is what you must do. Maybe at this moment the waves are pounding you, the winds are against you, and you feel like you are going under. Maybe a legion of troubles stands in your path. Maybe you feel like Jesus is silent and asleep, as he was for me that night in the back of the boat. But listen to me. *You are going to be alright ... if you are with Jesus.*

Will the storms in your life immediately cease? Probably not. Will that legion of troubles immediately flee from you? Unlikely. Nevertheless, you are going to be alright. What will you do? You will put one foot before the other and keep moving forward. You will make it through this day and the next. You will make it with the love, the strength, and the guidance of the one whom the wind and waves obey. You will not go through this storm alone.

And, if the worst should happen – yes, even if the worst should happen! – you are still going to be alright. Here is what I learned that night on the open sea. Those of us on that boat with Jesus had no guarantees that we would not perish in the storm. It might have been God's will to keep us safe by calling us home to heaven, rather than stilling the storm. Yet, even if we perished in the waves, plunging deep down to death itself, would we not be perfectly alright? *When you travel with Jesus, even death is nothing but a door to heaven and a portal to paradise.* Jesus! The wind and waves obey him! Legion bows to him! Death cowers before him!

Are you facing a storm? Don't know what to do? Don't know where to start? Friend, listen to my advice: Get in the boat. This is the most important decision you will ever make. I know that you are worried and fearful. I know that you feel anxious and overwhelmed. But you are going to be alright.

For Jesus is more powerful than your storm.

Key Discovery
Get in the boat.

Part Two

Entry 4
A Desperate Dad

Six weeks pass. The sun-drenched New England summer gives way to a cold, grey autumn. The dry, shriveled leaves outside my window drop silently from the branches with each movement of the wind. I have not experienced any similar episodes. Not a one. In fact, I am beginning to wonder if I just imagined the whole thing. After all, what I experienced was impossible, right? Maybe it was a "one time only" mental short-circuit. No doubt self-correcting. Nothing to be alarmed about.

It is a dim, drizzly Saturday morning, and I am up early. I pour myself a cup of coffee, let the dogs out, and putter about the kitchen for a moment. It will probably be awhile before anyone else is up and I enjoy these quiet moments. I take a sip of coffee, grab the television remote, and flip on the morning news to see if anything of interest has happened overnight. *"And in related news,"* reports the morning news anchor, *"White House sources have confirmed ..."*

At that moment, it hits me like someone intentionally upending the floor I'm standing on, like I'm riding a roller coaster, reaching the crest, now plunging downward. In a frightening moment of complete instability, I feel myself plunging forward, reaching for something solid to hold on to. A split second later, the grey morning light has given way to golden afternoon sun.

I am in Galilee.

I'm back.

It is as if someone has suddenly pulled up the shades in a darkened bedroom and now sunlight streams in. I feel the baking heat of the Mediterranean sun on my skin. Hungry gulls cry out as they circle over the docks. I smell the brackish air and see the sapphire sea sparkling with diamonds of sunlight.

I turn and see Peter running up. "Where've you been?" he asks impatiently.

I wonder, *Do you mean: For the past six weeks?*

Before I can figure out an appropriate answer, he continues: "You must have gotten separated from the group. Things got pretty wild when we ran into Legion this morning."

So, it's the same day here. For me, six weeks have passed; here, perhaps six hours.

Peter points. "We're over there. See that big crowd? Jesus is at the center of that. When we got back this morning, people were already gathering down by the docks waiting for us. They were expecting us."

We make our way into the teaming throng of people, pushing and squeezing, trying to work our way from the outer edge of the crowd to the center. We're trying to get closer to Jesus, who stands at the center ring of this circus.

Of course, this is easier said than done. Unfortunately, everyone else seems to have the same idea. They all want to get closer to Jesus. The result is an army of people pressing in on him from every side. Some bring children for Jesus to bless; others lurch forward on crutches, longing for help or healing; too many have no sense of those around them and launch into long, detailed explanations of their troubles.

Just then, there is a stir on the outer edge of the crowd. People begin to step aside, making way for a prominent member of the community. The man, winded and red-faced from running, frantically pushes aside anyone who will not get out of his way. Distraught, he throws himself at the feet of Jesus.

Peter is alarmed. He takes hold of my arm and says, "I know him! He's the ruler of the synagogue. He supervises the services here in Capernaum, choosing the participants and overseeing everything. His name is Jairus … and he's a good man." Peter adds: "I wonder what has him so upset?"

Jairus presses his forehead to the ground, showing Jesus the honor due a visiting king. The gesture is not lost on the crowd – the ruler is bowing before the carpenter. Then, peering up with desperate eyes, the words spill out of him: "Sir, it's my little daughter. She's dying. Please come and put your hands on her so that she will be healed and live."

Jesus reaches out his hand and pulls Jairus to his feet. "Take me to her."

"Please hurry!" Jairus urges, as they begin pressing through the crowd. "She's my only child, my little sweetheart, my princess. Every breath she takes seems weaker and weaker. We must not delay!"

Then, pushing through the crowd which is tightly packed around Jesus, Jairus pleads, "Please, please! Let us through! It is an emergency!"

Jairus propels himself forward. Jesus matches him pace by pace. They leave the waterfront and quickly make their way up the sloping streets toward the home of Jairus, perched on the high ground near the synagogue. The great crowd surges through the narrow lanes, flowing forward with Jesus. As the streets narrow, the crowd is almost crushing him.

Jairus pushes forward, leading the way. His urgency spills over with every step. He pleads: "All medical help has failed. My little girl is sinking away into death, and even the time it takes me to bring you to her may be too long. Please! She may be gone before we even reach her!"

Suddenly, Jesus stops dead in his tracks.

"Who touched me?" he asks, turning around.

Jairus continues to plow ahead, not realizing that Jesus has stopped. Jesus repeats himself: "Someone touched me."

I watch everyone back away from Jesus. "It wasn't me …. I didn't touch you …. I didn't do anything to you!"

Peter argues, "Who *hasn't* touched you? People are crowding around you, touching you and pressing against you on every side!"

But Jesus holds firm: "Someone touched me. I know that power has gone out from me."

After an awkward moment of silence, a young woman in the crowd takes a deep breath and steps forward. She is pale and thin, her face gaunt. Tired, dark circles ring her eyes. Trembling, she falls at the feet of Jesus. "It was me," she admits with embarrassment.

Then the words begin to spill out of her: "I've been sick, so sick – twelve years, just bleeding continually – twelve years, and no one could heal me ..."

I watch the crowd visibly draw back from her, creating a small empty island in the middle of a sea of people. The act is instinctive. We know that, by law, she is unclean and anyone who even touches her will be unclean.

Unstopped, her river of words continues: "I've spent everything I have to live on, going from doctor to doctor. But no treatment has helped me. Instead I just keep getting worse." Her voice lowers to almost a whisper: "Even this is not the worst part. The worst part is that for twelve years – twelve lonely years – I have been shunned. I am unclean. My family must separate themselves from me. My husband cannot touch me. My children cannot hug me. I cannot even attend worship. I am alone." Her dark eyes pool up. "Alone."

Now that she is speaking freely, her words gush out in a torrent. "So, when I heard you were coming to Capernaum, I thought, *If I can just touch his clothes, I will be healed.* And so I came up behind you, Sir, and stretched out my hand. And, as soon as my fingers brushed over the tassel of your cloak, I felt something – something deep inside me. Immediately the bleeding stopped and I could feel in my body that I was finally freed from my suffering."

She sinks to the ground, lets out a long, low sob, and covers her face to hide her tears. Jesus kneels on one knee before the woman. Slowly, he places a hand upon her chin, gently lifting her face so that he can look into her eyes. "Daughter, your faith has healed you," he states tenderly. "Go in peace. You won't be troubled any longer."[3]

His touch signals to all that she is not unclean.

His tenderness shows that she is to be cherished like a treasured daughter.

His words of affirmation build her up in a way that begins to make up for the humiliation and emptiness of her lost decade.

Already, the color has returned to her face …

Entry 5
A Little Girl

Just then, my eyes are drawn to a commotion near Jairus. Jairus has turned back, returning to Jesus. Some men stand in front of him, blocking his way.

"We have just come from your house," one says. "I'm sorry, Jairus. It's over. Your daughter is dead. Don't bother the teacher any longer."

Jairus doubles over like he has been gut-punched. His face drains of color. His knees buckle beneath him. He needs to be supported by those on either side of him to remain upright.

Ignoring them all, Jesus grabs Jairus by the shoulders and locks eyes with him. "Jairus!" he commands. "Jairus! Listen to me! Don't be afraid. Just believe."

Jairus nods his head in agreement, daring to hope.

"Just keep on believing and, I promise you, everything will be alright."

"Peter, James, and John – you come with me." Jesus turns to the crowd. "The rest of you stay here."

Peter grabs my arm and motions with a jerk of his head that I should tag along.

In less than five minutes, we are at the home of Jairus. It is an impressive Roman villa with a sweeping view of the sea, pale white-washed walls, and a walled courtyard overlooking the street. As soon as we enter the courtyard, I am overcome with the drama of the moment. I have never experienced anything like this! Such emotion! Such commotion! From one end of the courtyard to the other, men and women are wailing and beating their chests, in the customary way of the Middle East. Distraught cries and howling shrieks fill the air. Men raise their arms imploringly, crying out toward heaven. Women collapse to the ground, throwing dust and dirt skyward. The mournful sounds of flutes pierce the air, courtesy of the musicians who've been hired for the funeral event. Professional mourners, with hair streaming wildly and heart-rending wails and bursts of sobs, stage their best performance. The prominence of the family and the loss of an only child call for the biggest demonstration of grief possible.

Friends and members of the extended family already gather inside the house and the courtyard and spill out into the street. It seems that all of Capernaum is here, ready to show respect to one of their leading families. As Jairus enters the courtyard, they begin to circle around him offering their condolences.

But Jesus will have none of this. In a voice that is supremely confident, maybe even confrontational, he tells the mourners that their demonstration is entirely out of place. There will be no funeral here this day and they are foolish if they act as if there shall be. "Stop wailing!" he tells them. "She is not dead. The poor child is only sleeping."

However taken aback the mourners are upon hearing such an absurd statement, they regroup quickly. "Don't be ridiculous!" they spit in his direction. "Napping? I'm afraid not! They have already finished preparing her body! She is to be placed in the tomb this very day before the sun goes down." The group explodes with cold, caustic laughter.

Undeterred, Jesus directs Jairus to bring him without delay to his daughter. He then orders everyone else to leave. Only the girl's parents and our small group – Peter, James, John, and myself – are permitted to follow Jesus into the girl's bedroom.

I am the last one to enter the room and I close the door behind me. It is very dark. A single candle burns by the girl's bedside. My eyes must adjust from the bright afternoon sunlight to the darkness of the room.

I see her. A young girl, perhaps twelve years old, lies on her back on a bed of fresh linen. Her skin is as white as alabaster and as cold as marble. Her unlined face looks sunken and sallow in the candlelight. She wears a clean white robe and her hands are folded over her heart. The sweet, overpowering smell of perfume and spices hangs in the air. Her mother has finished washing her and preparing her for the tomb.

Jesus approaches and stands over her bedside, his eyes filled with a mixture of love and sorrow. Then he reaches down and takes her hand in his – a small, soft, child's hand, cold and colorless, held tenderly in the cracked and calloused hand of a carpenter. One hand holds only death, the other only life.

"Little girl," calls Jesus firmly. "Get up!"

At once, her eyelids flutter and she inhales loudly, a sudden gasp which startles everyone in the room. She opens her eyes wide and looks about the candlelit room. "Mom? Dad?" she whispers, "why are you all here?"

Like a pink sunrise glowing brighter by the moment, I watch the rosy flush return to her face. She sits up, quickly swings her legs off the bed, and stands up easily. At once, her parents throw themselves on her, giving her unrestrained hugs.

At the same time, the love that cascades from Jesus spills out into the room, washing us all with an inexpressible joy.

"Well, Mom, I guess you'd better get this girl something to eat," directs Jesus. "The poor child must be hungry after the journey she's been on!" The whole room laughs and jumps into motion.[4]

Jesus turns to me, his smile bright. "Did you see the look on Jairus' face when his little girl's eyes opened?"

I return his smile.

"Love," Jesus says. "There's nothing like a father's love…"

Entry 6
A Fall Forward

"Let's tell the group of mourners waiting outside these doors that there will certainly not be any funerals in this family today!" announces Jairus. "I can't wait to see the look on their faces!"

I am closest to the door, so I hold it open for the others, as our beaming little group makes their way out of the room. I am the last to leave and as I step through the door …

I step into my kitchen.

That's it. Just like that. Just a split second of light-headedness, a slight disequilibrium, and I stumble home again, headlong through two millennia. The perfume-scented death chamber gives way to the quiet familiarity of my own coffee-scented kitchen. The distraught din of the mourners can no longer be heard – the last cry echoed into oblivion more than two-thousand years earlier. The joyful exhilaration of Jairus has passed – Jairus and all whom he loved were themselves laid to rest centuries ago.

The television news anchor continues. *"Sources close to the President have now revealed …"* I realize it is the same story that was being reported when I, for lack of a better word, "fell" into Galilee. I look at the clock over the stove. No time has passed. My absence is non-existent. There are no "lost minutes" to account for.

Quickly, I find some paper and begin to jot down my impressions. I will later transcribe these details into the journal I keep in my office. But I feel I must make note of my experience while it remains so tangible and accessible in my mind. I must get these thoughts down immediately.

What are my initial impressions? What did I take away from this experience? Something surprising! The truth is, I've been looking in all the wrong places for the answer to my problems; I've been searching in the wrong direction. There are three things which became apparent to me, which I need to pass along to you.

The first thing is this:

Life is about love.

I was there. I saw Jairus, overwrought with worry over his little girl's health. I saw Jairus' wife, crushed by her loss. I saw their joy rise up and explode like fireworks when their little girl was restored to them. And here is what I saw: Nothing was more important to them than that little girl. Not their shining villa. Not their prominence. Not their considerable wealth. Their little girl – that's what mattered.

Why? Because, when it comes down to it, life is about love.

In truth, most people live their entire lives without understanding what life is really all about. They exist year after year with no idea why they are here on this earth. They will tell you, "I just want to be happy." And people try many different ways to be happy.

Some look for happiness in *popularity*. Particularly when we are young and our self-image is unformed, we try to measure our worth by what we see reflected back to us in the eyes of others. If lots of people know our name, certainly this means that we are an important person! If lots of people like us, certainly this is undeniable proof that we are in every way okay! If lots of people speak well of us, certainly all must be well in our lives – so many people cannot possibly be wrong! The problem is, the voice of the crowd can turn quickly. Yesterday's hero can become today's zero. One rumor can poison your popularity. And even a vast sea of shallow relationships cannot provide the depth for which we yearn. In truth, no amount of attention around us can fill the emptiness within us.

Some look for happiness in *possessions*. We think if we can just make enough money, acquire enough toys, buy a big enough house, or accumulate enough to possess some level of security – why, then we will be happy. The problem is, all possessions eventually wear out. The thrill of the new car disappears just about as quickly as that "new car smell." And even the safest investments cannot keep one secure from the ravages of old age and eventual death. Eventually we all must surrender our possessions as we slip from this life into the next.

Others look for happiness in *pleasure*. Certainly another drink, another drag, another drug, or another destination vacation will make us happy! The problem is, every vacation comes to an end. Every thrill has a price tag. And every high has a downside. We continually need a bigger kick to get the same high. And soon we realize that with every "kick" comes a "kick back," a swift kick that stings more each time. Even the strong, young, beautiful body which brought us such pleasure will eventually wither with age. No, lasting happiness is not found in pleasure.

Still others look for happiness in *power* and *prestige*. I have known people to battle an entire lifetime to attain a title and a corner office. The problem is, there is always someone younger and hungrier snapping at our heels. And if, by chance, we are lucky enough to hold onto that office, the day of our retirement will inevitably find us. In the end, we may try to cling to the power and prestige which we have spent a lifetime amassing, but it will surely slip through our open hands as we slip from this world into the next.

Popularity, possessions, pleasure, power, and prestige – Jairus had it all! Popularity, possessions, pleasure, power, and prestige – Jairus would trade it all! He would trade it easily for the little girl he loved.

The stark truth is, popularity, possessions, pleasure, power, and prestige will all eventually be lost. Sadly, they will all inevitably slip from our hands. If acquiring these things was the very purpose for which we were created, my goodness, that would be sad indeed. For that would mean that God intentionally created us to be … well, "losers!"

My friend, you were not made to be a loser! Instead, the true key to lasting happiness is love. Love is the one thing that you can carry with you into eternity. Love is the one thing that grows even as you give it away. Love is the one thing you can never get too much of. My friend, open your eyes! *You were made to be a lover, not a loser!*

Here is the simple truth: Love is why God created you. Yes, you were created to be the focus of God's love and affection. In short, God made you to love you.

Consider this: Why did God create us in the first place? The answer: He wanted a family. To put it simply: God wanted to have children. Yes, it's true!

Surely you can understand this feeling. There comes a time in most people's lives when a powerful thought begins to enter their mind: *I think I want a baby. I think we should start a family.* Perhaps a part of us resists the idea. After all, children are expensive. They steal our freedom, privacy, and sleep. They create these awful messes, from dirty diapers to dented cars. We all know this. And yet … and yet … we want someone to love. And we want someone to love us back. We know that this love will make us feel complete.

Is this not exactly how God felt? God wanted someone to give His love to. God wanted someone who would love Him back. He knew that there would be messes to clean up. He knew His heart would often be happy and often be hurt. He knew there would be a steep price to pay. But God made us to love us.

And here is the astonishing thought that occurred to me that day: *Just as deeply and desperately as Jairus loved his little girl*

... God loves you and me. Yes, God loves you like a father loves a cherished child. God is on your side all the way. God's eyes light up whenever you enter the room. God thinks you are irreplaceable. You are God's much-loved child, and nothing will ever change that.

God was there in the delivery room on the day you were born and His face beamed with excitement and wonder. God watched with pride on your graduation day, saying, "I wouldn't miss it!" God smiled when you walked down the aisle and stood before His altar and made your promises to love and cherish another. Every time you cried, God's heart broke with you. Every time you succeeded, God felt the victory. God loves you like a father loves his own child, like Jairus loved his little girl.

Whether you have been aware of it or not, your life has always been completely enveloped in love. Even from the very start. Even to the very end. Think of it this way...

Once, long ago, you were a tiny baby in your mother's womb. You felt warm and safe, tucked beneath her heart. Then one day, without warning, you felt your world close in around you. You felt afraid and out of control. It was suddenly time for you to leave that safe, warm world. In a way which was completely beyond your own control, you were pushed through a dark tunnel toward a bright light.

But then, you entered a wonderful new world of light and color, of freedom and movement. And what was the very first thing you saw? You saw the most beautiful sight in the entire world: the eyes of your mother. They placed you in her arms and she wrapped you in love and held you tight.

You were enveloped in love from the very start.

One day, you will again feel your world closing in around you. Things will feel frightening and out of control. You will think, *But I like it here! I'm comfortable here! I don't want to go!* But the walls will press in around you and you will again be pushed through a dark tunnel toward a bright light. You will enter a new world, a wonderful new world of breathtaking light and spectacular color beyond anything you have ever imagined. And then you will see the most beautiful sight you have ever seen: the eyes of your Father. He will hold you in strong arms and hug you as his much-loved child. At that moment you will feel the same love Jairus' little girl felt when she awoke. And you will know this to be true: God loves you like a father loves his cherished child.

Count on it. *Life is about love.* Maybe you think this is obvious. Maybe you think this is cliché. But it is absolutely true.

Sadly, most of us live our entire lives as if we only half-believe this big, beautiful, basic truth. If we truly, honestly, believed this – if we believed this with our whole heart, mind, and soul – oh, how different our lives would look! Suddenly, how we greet the woman working at the cash register would become an exercise of utmost importance. Suddenly, connecting with a friend after church would become as much an act of worship as connecting with God through Holy Communion. Suddenly, we would become consumed with thoughts of how to delight, support, and serve our spouse rather than consumed with how to serve our career.

Yes, I guess it does sound like an old cliché. *Life is about love.* But there is a reason it's an *old* cliché, rather than a *dead* cliché.

Because … it's true!

Therefore, to increase the joy and satisfaction in your life, learn to love and enjoy the people around you each day. Even now, in the middle of the storm, this will bring joy and laughter into your life. Even now, when life has knocked you down, this is the sure way to pull yourself back up.

In short, life is about love.

The second thing I observed is this:

Life is empty without love.

Never was this truth more obvious to me. When I looked into the eyes of the woman Jesus healed, this realization came crashing over me like never before. What part of her long illness most deeply impacted her? Was it that she was on the brink of financial ruin, having spent all she had to live on going from one doctor to another? Was it the frustration of twelve long years of unanswered prayers, of disappointing medical results, of things getting slowly worse rather than better? Was it the illness itself, the slow debilitating pull downward as it weakened and consumed her?

No, what most crushed this woman was the utter and complete break from human contact. It was the iron wall of separation from her friends, the chatter in the marketplace, the sharing in the synagogue. It was the insurmountable distance between herself and her husband, the unassailable chasm between herself and her own children.

Listen to her words: "The worst part is that for twelve years – twelve lonely years – I have been shunned. I am unclean. My family must separate themselves from me. My husband cannot touch me. My children cannot hug me. I cannot even attend worship. I am alone."

I will never forget her dark eyes filling with tears as she said that final word: "Alone." And I will never forget the wave of joy that washed over her when one simple touch brought the possibility of love back into her life.

Perhaps Jesus thought of this woman when he was later asked what is most important in life. A group of religious teachers one day came to question him. "What is the greatest commandment of them all?" they asked. "What is most important?" Without hesitation, Jesus answered, "Love the Lord your God with all your heart, soul, mind, and strength. And there is something else which is equally important: Love your neighbor as yourself."[5]

Do you hear the common word there? Love! Love God with everything in you – and love the people around you like you yourself would like to be loved.

Such an emphasis should not surprise us! God made us to love us. We are here on this earth because God wanted a family. We were wired from the very start for one primary purpose: to give and receive love!

For this reason, a life without love is a wasted life. We will, naturally, feel empty. We will feel off-center. We will feel disconnected. We will feel drained. Understandably! How could we possibly feel otherwise? We are not living a life aligned with the very purpose for which we were created!

Do you need still more proof of this? Perhaps irrefutable scientific proof? Some time ago I read about a series of odd experiments conducted by a professor at the University of Wisconsin. As a young, up-and-coming psychologist, Dr. Harry Harlow set out to study the I.Q. of rhesus monkeys. One day he noticed that the baby monkeys were developing a rather strange attachment to the soft terry cloth materials lining the bottom of their wire cages. They would lie on the cloth, cuddle with it, and even react violently if the terry cloths were removed. This led Harlow to conjecture that, in absence of their mothers, the infant monkeys were bonding to the soft, warm cloths that lined their cages.

To further explore the nature of this bonding, Harlow created elaborate wire creatures that resembled monkey mothers and attached a bottle to each. To his surprise, the infant monkeys preferred a soft, cuddly cloth to a cold, wire monkey that offered a bottle at which the little monkey could nurse.

Prior to this, the widely held belief was that babies love their mothers first and foremost because their mothers feed them.

After Harlow's groundbreaking study, scientists began to see that love – cuddling, connecting, and nurturing – were more valued by infants than even food itself.

We are wired from the very start to give and receive love.

Similar discoveries have been made with human babies. When the Soviet Union collapsed and visitors were again allowed behind the Iron Curtain, investigators were shocked to find orphanages where infants were warehoused by the thousands. In many cases, the only human contact these children experienced was to be fed and have their diapers changed. They were rarely held, rocked, or cuddled. As a result, many of these children were mentally and physically underdeveloped and many died from emotional neglect.

In short, they died from a lack of love.

Life is about love.

And life is empty without love.

But there is good news:

It's not too late for love.

It's not too late for love … and it's not too late for *you*.

God loves you and wants to treat you like a favorite child! There need be no shortage of love in your life. Ever. God will happily pour His love into your life.

Perhaps you are thinking, *I don't feel like I deserve it. I don't feel like I'm worthy of that kind of love.* But that is what God's amazing grace is all about. None of us deserves it. It's a free gift.

Perhaps you wonder, *But, after all my failures, maybe God changed His mind about me.* My friend, you are not a surprise to God. God is not up in heaven scratching His head saying, "What did I get myself into? I never dreamed he'd have that problem. I never imagined she'd have so many weaknesses." God made you. He knows everything about you. And He still loves you. You may have your faults, but you, my friend, are still His much-loved child. Let yourself be loved!

Maybe you have been deeply hurt. You feel like something has shut-down on the inside. You are thinking, *Jeff, I just feel dead inside. I have nothing left to give.* Or, *I've been hurt too many times. I won't open myself up to that again.* Perhaps your wall is self-imposed: you've built an iron wall around yourself to keep from getting hurt again.

My friend, it's time for that wall to come down. The same Jesus who brought love into the life of that long-weakened woman can bring love into your life. The same Jesus that brought a little girl back to life can bring new life to you.

Do you feel dead inside? The Lord of Life is with you right now. He will enter your darkness just as he entered the dark, candlelit room of that lifeless little girl. He will not listen to the critics and complainers. Neither should you. He will not give up on you. Neither should you. Instead, just as he did for that little girl, he will tenderly take your hand into his own.

Can you feel his hand upon you? Even now, as you read this? It's time for you to experience a resurrection of the heart. In your mind, picture the feel of his hand on yours. Feel the calloused hand of the Carpenter of Galilee. Feel the gentle hand of a friend. Even if your heart feels dead, even if you cannot think of a word to say to him, he has a word to say to you.

"I love you."

The Lord of Love is inviting you to re-claim your rightful place in his family.

How will you respond?

Say, "Yes!" Be like that woman who got just as close as she possibly could to Jesus, reaching out her hand to touch even his cloak. Reach out to him. He is the epicenter of love and life. He is what your heart has been yearning for.

Do you need a hug? When one of his children gives you a hug – that's from him. Do you need encouragement? When one of his preachers climbs into the pulpit with a Bible in his hand and a message in his heart – that's from him. Do you need a kind word? When an old friend just happens to call – that's from him.

Yes, God loves you like a father loves his own cherished child. And your Father has a million different ways to hug you, encourage you, and love you each day.

There should be no lack of love in your world. God's people are everywhere around you. Doubt it? Find a good-old, love-filled, Bible-based church. Join his family. Meet his kids. Let God love you.

Key Discovery
Let God love you.

Part Three

Entry 7
A Golden Day

"Your cousin is dead."

The news jolts Jesus.

"How?" someone asks. "How did it happen?"

Jesus already seems to know.

We fire questions at the men who have just arrived in Capernaum. They bring with them the latest news: the bloody tale of the death of John the Baptist at the hands of Herod, the despised Rome-backed king of Galilee.[6] While we fill the room with questions and speculation, Jesus remains silent. Perhaps he is thinking of his own approaching death. It is now just before Passover. Jesus will die during the Passover, one year from now.

A feeling of foreboding hangs over me. I sense death's silent but unrelenting approach. Each day it creeps a step closer. Death's latest strike, hitting so close to home, has the entire group rattled. But Jesus alone knows the exact timeline … Death will collide head-on with our group this time next year.

"We should take a break," Jesus offers. Lately there have been so many people coming and going, Jesus rarely even takes time to eat. He looks about the room. "Come with me. We'll find a quiet place and get some rest. Just us. No crowds."[7]

The idea immediately changes the mood in the room. At once we're on our feet, bustling about the house, gathering up our things. We'll head down to the wharfs, Jesus explains, and use one of the fishing boats owned by Peter to cross from our base of operations here in busy Capernaum to the beautiful lonely lands on the northeast coast.

A wave of fierce anxiety sweeps through me as I remember my last experience in that boat crossing the Sea of Galilee. I think of the stormy night, the terrifying darkness, and the furious waves. Then I think of Jesus, the look of him standing in the stern scolding the waves like a parent scolds an unruly toddler. Once again, I will be sailing with the one whom the wind and waves obey.

With a confident smile and a peaceful heart …

I will get in the boat.

It may be the most beautiful day I have ever experienced.

The sun hangs high in the sapphire sky, warming me and washing the world with gold. A light breeze moves through the lush green grass, sending silent waves across the endless sea of meadows. Small birds dart about overhead, filling the morning with their song. Below me stretches the mirrored expanse of the sea, glittering like a blue diamond. There is nothing in the world comparable to the beauty of an early spring day in the Galilean foothills. No wonder they called this the Promised Land.

We sit on either side of Jesus, relaxing in the soft grass, gazing absently at the sea. Earlier, Jesus had poured his heart out to us. He spoke not only of his cousin John, he spoke of the future. He spoke of a coming kingdom, a kingdom I could scarcely imagine. He spoke simply and clearly and confidently – so simple were his words that I wondered why I had never seen things quite this way before. When Jesus spoke of his Father, the mysteries of eternity seemed fairly plain and obvious. When he spoke of heaven, he spoke as one who had walked the streets. Often I glanced over at Peter, John, and the others, as they hung upon his words. When they would turn and catch my eye, they would nod as if to say, "Of course! How did we not see it before?"

After a couple of quiet hours, most of us are beginning to nod off. After days of constant pressure and action, it feels good to lie back in the grass, soak in the warmth of the early spring sun, and shut our eyes. I lay on my back, looking up into the cloudless sky. I think of my wife; I think of my kids.

Just then Peter shoots straight up and says, "What in the world?" The obvious tone of puzzlement, even alarm, causes us all to stir at once. With hands over our eyes to shield them from the sun, we stare down into the valley below.

An enormous crowd of people – hundreds; no, maybe thousands strong – are making their way toward us. The mass of humanity moves like a ragtag army, marching steadily forward with one goal in mind. They come to see Jesus. They cross the long, flat, grassy plain that hugs the shoreline. Some are helped along on crutches; others are carried. Most walk with entire families – children, parents, and grandparents, aunts and uncles, nieces and nephews. Sometimes an entire village walks together as one, all eager to see Jesus, touch Jesus, have a piece of Jesus.

Evidently word has gotten out that we have been on the move. As we made our way to this location by boat, people began to run along the shoreline, eager to catch up with us. As they ran, they spread news of our whereabouts to each village along the way. Soon people were draining out from every corner of the region, an unstoppable river of humanity streaming in our direction. They come from a hundred hidden hamlets and unnamed crossroads; from the uncounted farming villages of the interior and the teaming trading posts that dot the coast. Within hours, the crowd swells to over twenty-thousand. And still they come.

It is a sight that melts the heart of Jesus. Though he had hoped to withdraw from the public and be alone with us for a time, he is visibly moved at the sight of all these people who have so rapidly and earnestly followed him. I see the change come over him. It hits him with the force of a blow to the stomach. Jesus lets out a loud, low groan. "Look at them. I ache for them. They are like sheep without a shepherd."

Jesus looks out over the massive crowd. Watching his eyes, I think to myself: He does not see merely a mass of nameless people. He sees individuals, individuals who are infinitely loved and infinitely valued. He sees men who have at times made heaven laugh, women who have made heaven hurt, and children who make heaven hope. Every face has a name and every name has a story.

Yet the eyes of Jesus also see that sheep without a shepherd stray helplessly and are bound to perish. He sees the fate of these people unless they are shepherded. And so Jesus makes the decision to shepherd them.

He turns to us and simply states: "They're going to need us. Let's go."

We begin making our way down the sun-washed meadows toward the blue-diamond sea. Soon the sheep will meet their shepherd.[8]

It doesn't take long for someone to recognize us. "There!" someone shouts. "It's him! That's Jesus!" People run toward us, eager to be the first to speak with him. Jesus, without hesitation, wades deep into the sea of humanity. People swirl around him, filling every available space, like seawater filling the holes left by a child digging in the sand at the surf's edge. Jesus will address the crowd, but first he will attend to their sick.

Peter immediately begins issuing instructions, directing each of us to take our places in a protective circle around Jesus lest he be crushed by the crowd. Leadership comes naturally to Peter. I've noticed this. I'm not sure anyone ever asked him to organize our efforts. He just seems to be the type that is comfortable speaking up, directing others, and being in charge. We, on the other hand, naturally bend to his leadership. His skills are well-honed from a lifetime running a business, managing employees, and directing fishing crews. Now Peter's natural strength and skill is focused on protecting Jesus and facilitating his ministry. Peter begins organizing people into some semblance of a line, so they might each have a moment with Jesus in a relatively fair and orderly fashion.

I watch as Jesus meets each individual. I study him. I am fascinated by him. He is unlike any individual I have ever met. The best way I can describe it is this: He radiates love. Yes, that's it. As the sun radiates light, Jesus radiates love. It is his very nature. For Jesus to meet someone and not love them would be as unnatural as the morning sun rising in the sky only to cast darkness upon us. The sun can't help shining, and Jesus can't help loving. It's who he is. It's what he does. It is at the very core of his personality. This is the key to what most people refer to as his charisma.

Take the family he speaks to now. They are a young family: a simple peasant who works the land, together with his very young wife who holds their first child in her arms. They come to Jesus because their little one labors at his breathing. As they step before him, Jesus reaches out his hand to clasp the hand of the young man in a friendly, familiar greeting.

I watch the hand of Jesus. I watch closely. As the young man tells his story, I marvel at the way he uses that hand to communicate. He shakes the man's hand firmly with his right hand, while placing his left hand gently on his elbow, drawing him closer and expressing friendship and warmth. A moment later, his hand moves upward. He rests it upon the young man's shoulder to show that he is listening, he cares, he is connected. Still later, he claps the young man's upper arm heartily as they break into laughter.

The hand of Jesus – it is the calloused hand of a carpenter; it is the gentle hand of a caregiver – it is the hand of one who not only builds *things*, it is the hand of one who builds *people*. He gestures with his hand, and heals with his hand, and blesses with his hand. In the end, he reaches out his hand to tenderly touch the heaving chest of that little one. Instantly, the infant's struggling little lungs begin to rise and fall with ease. The young mother's eyes fill with tears and her husband's heart fills with gratitude.

As the young family moves on, the next family finds that it is their turn to be with Jesus. They begin to tell him about their constant trouble with their aging mother's eyesight. I look now at the eyes of Jesus. They are expressive eyes, glittering sometimes with emotion, flashing sometimes with intensity, bright most often with joy. When Jesus meets someone, he focuses his eyes upon that person as if there is not another person in this entire world more interesting or captivating. He now gives his undivided attention to the family before him. Turning to the aged woman, he places his hand over her pale, rheumy eyes. He speaks a word of blessing. As he removes his hand, astonishingly the ancient woman looks through new eyes, bright, strong, and young.

In the hours that follow, one after another comes to Jesus. One after another shares his story, presents her need, hungers for a moment with Jesus. Jesus focuses on each one as if there is but one. Indeed he loves each one as if he has no one else to love.

The sun hangs low on the horizon. I'm tired; I'm hungry; I've had enough. And I'm getting annoyed. I'm annoyed that people just keep coming, in an endless parade of selfishness. Can't they see that we're tired? Can't they see that Jesus is only one man? They think only of themselves.

And I'm beginning to note a trend. A fair percentage of the people who now line up to meet Jesus have no particularly urgent need. Many simply want Jesus to bless their children.

Irritated, I can hold my silence no longer. With far more harshness in my voice than I intend, I release the irritation that has been building within me. "Listen, everyone! He can't possibly speak with all of you. There are too many of you!" I turn to the young families which group around us. "You need to stop bringing your children to bother Jesus."

At once Jesus turns to face me directly. His dark eyes blaze with indignation. I have never seen Jesus angry before. Now his anger flashes in my direction and I shrivel within, like an unwatered plant shrivels in the scorching summer sun. My face burns with embarrassment.

"Let the children come to me," he says forcefully, "and don't do anything to stop them." He looks around the group, speaking loud enough now for all of us to hear. "Don't ever get between me and them. For the Kingdom of God belongs to those who are like these little children."

Jesus tousles the curly black hair of a little boy, whose face beams up at him with affection. "Look at these faces! They trust me! They love me! How could I not love them? I'll tell you this much, you've got to be just like these children in order to get into the Kingdom of God."

Before I have a chance to respond, Jesus scoops up a toddler into his arms and hugs him tightly, pretending to squeeze the air out of him. "Love you, kiddo!" Then, looking about at all the little ones eagerly grouped around him, Jesus announces, "Okay, guys, bring it on!"

At once, a dozen children release their parent's hand and run to Jesus, throwing their arms around him, clinging to his legs, and holding out their arms to be picked up. With an exaggerated look of fear, Jesus pretends to be tackled to the ground. Giggling, shouting toddlers throw themselves on Jesus, climbing all over him. One little boy he lifts soaring into the air over his shoulders, as the boy pretends to fly. Another he seats upon his shoulders, as if seated upon a throne. As the boy looks down at his parents from his lofty perch, Jesus asks him if he intends to be that tall when he is all grown up. One after another, little ones dissolve into laughter, as Jesus teases, tickles, and plays.

Finally, breathless from his romp, Jesus sits back upon a large rock that forms a rough-hewn seat in the midst of the grassy meadow. A little girl snuggles onto his lap, as her proud parents look on in delight. Other children find a seat in the grass, grouping around Jesus' feet. He asks one boy what he would like to be when he grows up, then listens with great interest. He asks another youngster about his puppy and still another about her brother. Then Jesus begins to speak seriously to them, speaking of God's Kingdom and their place in it.

At last he turns to me. "Do you want to show your love for me? Do you want to do something nice for me? Honestly?" For a second, our eyes meet. The playful Lord is suddenly very serious. "If you want to show love to me, just show love to one of these little ones."[9]

Entry 8
An Empty Stomach

The sun sinks low, sending flecks of gold across the sea. Soon it will slide beneath the horizon. It's been a long day and I can think of little else but the throbbing ache in my feet and the gnawing emptiness in my stomach. I haven't had anything to eat since breakfast in Capernaum twelve hours earlier. I'm tired; I'm hungry; I wish I was home. The same is probably true for the thousands who surround us. Worse still, while I enjoyed a relaxing morning on a boat and a quiet hillside, the multitudes around me spent those hours in a frantic race to catch up to Jesus. They've been on their feet for hours. Some must be near collapse. I know I am.

Something has to be done. I move over to Peter and motion for a couple of others to join us. We huddle in a tight circle. "What's the plan here?" I inquire impatiently. No one answers. "Soon it will be dark and these people have had nothing to eat all day." The disciples and I cannot understand why Jesus is holding the people here so long. Our uneasiness grows until we feel we must act if he doesn't.

We decide to approach Jesus as a group. We will urge him to dismiss the crowd immediately. Peter speaks for us: "We're out here in the wilderness and it's getting late. Send the crowds away so they can go to the nearby farms and villages and buy themselves some food."

Jesus levels his gaze at us. "You feed them."

Peter looks over to us with raised eyebrows, then back to Jesus.

"Are you serious? With what?" Peter asks. "It would take a small fortune to buy food for all these people!"

But Jesus is quite serious. "What *do* you have? Go and find out."

We turn and wade into the crowd, making inquiries. Yet, when we return to Jesus a short time later, we have little to show for the effort. Only Andrew locates so much as a morsel to eat. "I found a little boy with five loaves of bread," he reports, "plus two fish."

We think that Jesus will now see the impossibility of keeping the crowd here with him any longer. What could even Jesus do with such a tiny bit of food? We feel sure he will now, without further delay, pronounce a benediction over them and hurry them off.

Instead, to our consternation, Jesus instructs the crowd to be seated. Word sweeps through the multitude and they begin to lower themselves to the ground. The process is orderly; the people are arranged in groups, some groups numbering as few as fifty, others numbering nearly one-hundred, with lanes in between, so that we might serve the food. Many recline leisurely in the soft grass like wealthy Romans reclining at a banquet table. Others lean forward with anticipation, craning their necks eagerly to see what Jesus might have in mind. They are hungry. They hope to be fed. The sense of expectation is palpable.

Our feeling is quite the opposite. Ours is a sense of growing dread. Thousands are being asked to get ready to dine – on five loaves and two fish! How in the world can Jesus even imagine that this will end well? The crowd has swollen to more than twenty-thousand!

Andrew calls to the little boy, who eagerly brings his little lunch forward to share with Jesus. His simple loaves are not large, golden loaves, meant to feed an entire family. Rather they are small flat cakes, sprinkled with barley, the food of the poorest of the poor. Like many in this region, the boy also carries with him a couple of dried fish. The fish will serve as a humble compliment to the little loaves, making the coarse barley a bit more palatable. It is the food of the Galilean poor, but Jesus welcomes it.

Taking the little lunch in his hands, Jesus lifts his face skyward, offering a simple prayer of thanks. Then, taking the bread in both hands, he begins to break it and distribute it piece by piece to his disciples, who will in turn distribute it to the hungry multitude.

I watch as an amazing thing begins to happen. I watch carefully, intently, hungrily, my heart racing, my stomach burning. Jesus breaks the little loaves in two, then in two again, and yet again. He does the same with the fish. He hands pieces to each disciple to place in simple wicker baskets which can be passed easily through the crowd. Yet, here is the astonishing thing! As often as Jesus divides the little boy's lunch, there always seems to be more!

The disciples head off in every direction, circulating through the crowd. As the baskets are passed among the hungry multitude, each takes as much as they desire. Fathers ensure that each family member has a portion; mothers break up the bread and divide the fish evenly among each of their children. The baskets are passed from family to family, from one end of the multitude to the other, from the gentle slope of the foothills to the sandy expanse of the shoreline. Yet the supply never reaches an end!

I accompany Peter as he carries his basket from group to group. In the first group, a hungry young father takes so much bread for his family that I can't imagine there can be much of anything remaining for those who follow. But the next family does the same, helping themselves until they are completely satisfied. It continues like this to the far reaches of the vast crowd, a sea of famished faces looking up at us, acre after acre of hungry humanity. Yet all eat their fill.

In the end, we gather up the leftovers, collecting the odd pieces and unused portions again in our baskets. Regrouping with Jesus, we discover that we have collected exactly twelve baskets full of extra food – twelve! One basket for each disciple! I smile when I think that Jesus not only supplied the needs of the multitude, he has provided perfect care for his disciples as well. Yes, in caring for others, they will have their own needs met as well.

As I see the bread and inhale its earthy aroma, my stomach growls. My mouth waters and I swallow hard. Each of the twelve has been provided for. The great multitude has been provided for.

Only two people will go hungry.

Only Jesus and I have no bread to fill our empty stomachs.

Yet, without being told, a beautiful thing begins to happen. The twelve quietly bring their baskets to us. They lay down their baskets in front of Jesus and me. We reach into the baskets, hungry and happy. A smile lights every face, a smile as bright and innocent and wonder-filled as the smiles that lit the faces of the children. Jesus, who created this bounty, has provided his disciples with an opportunity to share from their overflowing baskets of blessings.

From all that he gives ... they are privileged to give back to him.[10]

Entry 9
A Windswept Hill

Now, with stomachs full and eyes drowsy, we soak in the last of the sunlight. Around us, the great crowd is beginning to stir.

"Peter, gather up the men at once and leave immediately for Bethsaida," orders Jesus. "I'll meet up with you there."

For some reason, Jesus is suddenly on edge. Without delay, we regroup and prepare for the short walk down to the boat. "Just a minute," Jesus says. "Jeff, you stay with me."

Once again my face flushes with embarrassment. I feel like there is tension that exists between Jesus and me right now. I know that I let my impatience get the best of me earlier and I lashed out at a bunch of children. I figure Jesus wants to hash this out further.

Instead, Jesus takes me into his confidence, telling me something he hasn't told the others. "This situation could turn on us," Jesus confides. "Be prepared." There is no fear in him, just urgency. "There is a group of men here who are plotting to kidnap me tonight as soon as darkness settles in."

"What? For what purpose?" I question with growing alarm.

"They intend to make me their king, with or without my consent. Tonight the plot will be launched. They'll try to capture me and carry me into Jerusalem in a grand, royal procession, sweeping the capital off its feet during the Passover festival. The city will be packed with thousands of visitors – and totally on edge. They want to use me to ignite a riot and jump-start a revolt against Rome. And these men – let's just say, they're very determined."[11]

"What are you going to do?" I interrupt.

"Jeff, you begin dismissing the crowd. We need to break this up right away before it gets out of control. Start spreading the word. While they are watching *you*, I will slip off into the hills."

"Then what?" I ask.

"Then come find me. Take the road that heads north, winding up into the hills. You will find me. I'll be watching for you."

Late that night, I am making my way alone along a deserted road. My breathing is hard, as the road snakes its way up through the hills. The chirping of crickets and katydids fills the night. The slow, tired crunch of my feet on the gravel seems an unnatural interruption to their din. It is their world now. It is night.

I hope I'm on the right road. I've never been here before. There's been no sign of Jesus. My eyes focus downward, watching the path immediately in front of me, lest I stumble in the darkness. But, as I reach the crest of the hill, a breathtaking vista suddenly unfolds before me. Far below me is the sea, black and impenetrable. Above me is a sky that is alive with glittering stars and fast-moving clouds, dramatically back-lit by the moon. A storm is on its way. The clouds race through the star-strewn sky, charging toward the sea. The enormous Passover moon ducks in and out from behind the clouds.

Just then, as the near-full moon slips from behind a cloud, moonlight washes over the hilltop. I see a solitary figure. He sits alone along a rocky crag, hands clasped, eyes peering out over the tossing sea. Now I watch as he lifts his head skyward and begins to speak. Earnestly. Emotionally. Pleading.

It is Jesus. He pours out his heart to his Father, here on this lonely mountaintop. I don't want to disturb him. This seems too private a moment. I stand still where I am, not moving, not making a sound. I want to hear Jesus, hear how the Prince of Heaven speaks to his Father.

I am able to make out only one word.

I hear the word several times.

It is the word … *"Abba."*

It is the same word the little ones who played with Jesus earlier today used when speaking to their dads. It is the simplest and most common term used in a loving family. *"Abba."* It means, *"Daddy."*

So this is how the greatest theological mind of all time speaks to the divine.

This is how the eternal Word conjugates his perfect prayer and praise.

"Daddy." [12]

Jesus looks in my direction and motions for me to come and take a seat beside him. We sit together in silence for a moment. Jesus is the first to speak. "Jeff, are we alright here? Is there something you want to say to me?"

I stumble for a reply. I haven't rehearsed this. Even with my long, lonely walk to Jesus, even with all that quiet time on my hands, I still haven't fully framed the words. My feelings toward Jesus are complex.

"Lord, you know all things. You know what is in my heart."

"Yes, but it's important for you to say it. *You* need to know it, too."

I look down at the ground. Then I begin to speak softly. "I'm sorry I got angry at those children. I'm sorry I lost my patience and lashed out like that," I mumble. "I thought I was doing it for you, but … but I guess I really was just thinking about my tired feet and hungry stomach and used-up patience."

I look up, ashamed. Jesus looks deep into my eyes. "Jeff, I didn't speak those tough words to you to make you feel bad. I spoke to you like that because I know you are better than that."

I draw in my breath sharply, hold it a second, then exhale slowly.

"Listen, Jeff, let's get one thing straight. I see things in you. I am your biggest fan. I believe in you more than you believe in yourself. And so, I will always keep pressing you to become the man I know you can become."

"Lord," I said, "Why me? Why all this special attention? Why am I even being brought here?"

"You are special to me. I see something in you."

At once, love sweeps over me. I thought I would feel uncomfortable, even belittled, having this talk with Jesus. Instead, I feel only acceptance. Just as the entire landscape around us brightens when the moon emerges from behind a cloud, my entire emotional world brightens when I am with Jesus.

I plunge on. "But, why am I here? When I'm here, I miss my wife, and I miss my kids and all my friends from home. But when I'm home, I miss you and Peter and John and the rest. Why is this happening to me?" I pause for a moment, then ask the question that frightens me: "What if I get stuck here?"

Jesus looks at me, his face serious. "Jeff, do you love me?"

"Yes, Lord, you know I do."

"Then follow me – follow wherever I lead you."[13]

As Jesus speaks these words, he looks deep into my eyes. Is there sadness in his eyes? Or just a depth of emotion that makes it difficult for either of us to find adequate words? Silently, Jesus reaches out his hand to place it reassuringly upon my shoulder.

As his hand presses upon my shoulder, I suddenly lose my balance. I careen forward, falling from that dark Galilean mountaintop …. Head over heals … Deep, deep … into the Twenty-First Century.

I slash through centuries and instantaneously land …

Beside Kathy.

Entry 10
A Desperate Talk

"Are you listening to me?"

"Yes, of course I'm listening," I say automatically.

Of course, I'm not *listening,* I think automatically. *Not at all. Not a word of it.*

I have no idea what my wife has just said. In fact, I don't even remember what the topic was – and Kathy knows this full well. She can see the deer-in-the-headlight look on my face.

At a complete loss, I blink and refocus my eyes on the new environment into which I have tumbled. I was gone this time for four days – my longest trip yet. My mind is completely filled with Galilee. I've talked with Jesus. I've watched the multitude being fed. I've laughed with my friends in Capernaum, sailed the diamond-blue sea, and hiked the rugged hills. Four days.

Yet, to Kathy, she and I are midstream in a conversation. My absence was not even noticeable, occupying the length of time needed to blink one's eye.

Kathy is trying to make a point, completing a sentence she began seconds earlier. But between this latest word and the one which preceded it, four days have passed in my experience. Four *incredible* days!

I feel disoriented, distracted, confused. And no wonder! The chain of events within which I have been existing for the past four days has been completely and utterly shattered – and then, by some invisible hand, this broken chain has been reattached to a completely different strand of time. And I'm left with some sort of strange time traveler's "hangover."

"Jeff, you're not paying attention."

What was your first clue?

I'm in my kitchen, facing down my wife, trying to mentally regroup. This is no small undertaking. Kathy is tiny – five feet tall at best. But she is tough – tough as Goliath. This little giant has the heart of a warrior.

But now this little giant of mine is broken. She is broken by four years of unrelenting economic recession, four years of slowly evaporating finances, four years of unremitting pressure. You see, Kathy is responsible for paying the bills for our family and for our ministry. And the bills are big ones. Our church must make a mortgage payment of nearly thirty thousand dollars *per month*. We must make a payroll for seventy employees. We must meet the material demands of two childcare centers, a church, and even a restaurant! Yes, we have experienced amazing growth over the years. But amazing growth has left us with an amazing need for financial support, a demand which is unyielding and merciless.

In past years this need has been satisfied primarily by the monthly tuition paid by those who send their children to our childcare centers. Yet, in recent years, as our nation sank deeper and deeper into the Great Recession, unemployment climbed higher and higher. As young parents lost their jobs, they lost their need for childcare. As the recession strangled our nation, our ministry's income evaporated month by month. Soon paying our mortgage became impossible. Next paying our utility bills, insurance, and overhead became unlikely. Finally, even providing a weekly paycheck for our staff became doubtful. As the Executive Director and Chief Financial Officer of our ministry, Kathy bears the brunt of this each day, writing the checks, juggling the constant demands, and fielding the unrelenting phone calls from creditors who want payment. As the recession drags on, Kathy drags down.

Add to this the *emotional* recession which engulfs us. This is the greatest of the recessions, as joy recedes and dreams wither. How many nights will we lie awake at three o'clock in the morning, rehearsing what we will say the next time we have to report to the bank that holds our mortgage? How many mornings will we awaken, wondering if this will be the day when the bank decides to foreclose on our property or the week when we cannot pay our employees? How many? How many times will we wonder if we should just give up, surrendering to those twin recessions of economics and emotion, finally counting our life's work a failure? How many?

Now Kathy stands in front of me, her hands held out toward me, palms up, imploring. "What are we going to do?"

I remain silent. I want to say something comforting. I want to offer a solution. But I have nothing. So I search for words.

Kathy continues on: "Jeff, neither of us has received a paycheck for more than four months. Four months! Our savings are wiped out. My checking account has, like, a hundred dollars in it."

"Things will get better. We made it through the summer. That's when things are always the toughest for a church. Now that fall is here it will get better."

Kathy's voice is full of weariness, full of exasperation. She's always the one who brings a common sense solution to every discussion. She's always the one to deal with problems without an ounce of drama. She's my rock. But, this time, she seems crushed. "We can't just bury our head in the sand. I can't keep hoping – and then being devastated when things don't turn around."

"I don't know what you want me to say," I mutter defensively. "Do you want to print out a budget report and I'll try to find something? I can go over the numbers again. I can take a stack of files home with me over the weekend."

I know I'm doing the "guy thing." I'm trying to fix her. I'm trying to rescue her. But I'm only creating more turmoil in myself, knowing that I'm setting myself up for failure. There is no magic solution that will suddenly pop out at me. We've been over and over these numbers. We long ago made every cut and found every efficiency that we could – short of locking the doors and walking away.

I try a different route. "Do you want me to just shut up and listen and try to understand what you're feeling, instead of trying to fix your feelings?" I move closer, thinking perhaps a hug would be welcome. "Listen, Kath, I don't know what to say here."

She just looks up into my eyes, despondent and disconsolate.

Then Kathy says something that I know must kill her: "Maybe we should sell our house." It was her dream house, the house she designed and custom built a decade earlier. "We can't afford the mortgage, and I'd rather be proactive. I'm afraid we'll lose everything."

Her words make me sick to my stomach. I feel like such a loser. Maybe I'm old-fashioned, but I've taken pride in being a good provider. I've worked hard, really hard. I've been successful, by any measure. But now, week after week, I can't even bring home a paycheck. I haven't provided a single cent. For months. And it tears at me.

A moment ago, I was with Jesus, just the two of us, face to face, on that craggy hillside overlooking the stormy sea. "You are special to me," he said. I believed him.

Then why is he letting me go through this? Hours earlier I saw him feed thousands. Why is he not providing for me? If Jesus cares as much as he claims he does, how come Kathy and I are hurting this way? How come our entire ministry, created in *his* name to do *his* work, faces imminent collapse? How come everything for which I have worked, prayed, and dreamed faces looming dismemberment?

If you care, Jesus, how come?

Entry 11
A Scribbled Page

I pull the notebook from my desk drawer, turn to the next empty page, and begin scribbling my thoughts. I slowly try to make sense of it all …

Here is what I have learned in life: When God does something that you *cannot* understand, fall back to what you *can* understand. So much of life is beyond my ability to understand. Especially now. Therefore, all I can do is fall back to what I do know. And here is what I know: God is love. God is good. God is just. His every action falls within these simple parameters. These are my certainties. And, in a world of uncertainty, I rest upon these certainties.

Therefore, while I cannot understand the difficulty I now find myself in, I rest upon the certainty that God is working in my life in a manner which is completely loving.

What difficulty are *you* wrestling with? A heartbreaking divorce? A crushing loss? A debilitating disease? Or, like me, are you wrestling with an impossible financial situation? If you're wrestling with an equally painful and confusing situation, the same is true for you as well. God will handle you in a way which is completely loving. You will see.

With this journal entry, I will record what made the strongest impression upon me during these past four days. I will battle my uncertainties and add depth to my certainties. Here is what I know. Here is what I have seen. Here is what I need *you* to see …

Your problem is not a problem.

My friend, Jesus is completely aware of your situation. He cares about what you are going through right now. He cares about your hungers and your needs. He is completely aware of what is happening in your life.

On that sunny spring day when Jesus fed the thousands, I assumed Jesus was unaware of our needs. We all assumed this. That is why we pressed him to move the crowd along quickly and dismiss them early. Yet, in reality, nothing could be further from the truth. Jesus was fully and completely aware of the needs of those around him. More importantly, he already possessed a plan for meeting those needs and the power to accomplish that plan.

Perhaps you would argue, "But, Jeff, you don't know how big my problem is!"

Is your problem bigger than trying to feed twenty-thousand? Is your situation more impossible than having only five loaves and two fish to bring to the table?

Let me tell you something: *Your problem is not a problem to Jesus*. Jesus already has the answer. That problem comes as no surprise to him. He is not up in heaven at this very moment, scratching his head, saying, "Holy Cow, I didn't see this coming!" That situation in your family, that financial difficulty, that disease which pummels your body – that problem does not have him baffled! Jesus was not caught unprepared two-thousand years ago by a crowd's need for food. Nor is he caught unprepared today by your needs. He knows every problem we're going to face. He knows every difficulty we're ever going to go through.

The good news is, Jesus already has the solution. He's in control. He's thought it through. He's working behind the scenes even when you can't see it. Goodness and love are following you all the days of your life. Whether you can see it or not, all things are working together for good in your life.[14] These are the promises of God and therefore God must act within these parameters in all His dealings with you.

During the final conversation I had with Jesus, alone on that windswept hillside, Jesus said these words to me: "You are special to me." My friend, he says the same to you. You are special to him. He sees something in you – something no one else sees.

Maybe you're thinking, *I'm just a housewife. I'm just a businessperson. I just stand behind a cash register.* No, you are not *just* anything. You are a child of the Heavenly Father. He created you to love you. You are a blessed person.

Perhaps you're thinking, *Me? Even me, with all my weaknesses? Even me, with all my problems? Even me, with all my sins?* Yes, even you! A parent does not for a minute stop caring about his child simply because that child begins to struggle. Nor does God! In fact, most parents put all the more time and effort into the child who struggles. That child receives all the more attention. And so it is with you.

You may not be perfect, but you are irreplaceable. Believe the words of Jesus. He speaks for his Father. He speaks for all the company of heaven. "You are special." That is why your needs will not for a moment go unnoticed.

Jesus is fully aware of your situation. And the good news is: Your problem is not a problem to Jesus. He already has a solution in mind.

There is another thing that Jesus showed me that afternoon. It is this:

The little things are the big things.

For many years, when my children were small, I had a large sign on my office wall which read, "A hundred years from now, it will not matter what my bank account was, the sort of house I lived in, or the kind of car I drove ... but the world may be different because I was important in the life of a child."

Those words hung directly over my desk, where I would view them a dozen times a day. It would remind me of the little ones who waited for me at home, eager for Daddy to walk through the door. It will now also remind me of what Jesus tried to teach on that beautiful spring afternoon by the Galilean Sea.

When Jesus lifted a child into his arms, I see now that he was taking the future in his hands. When Jesus made a child feel a little bit more loved, he made the future a little more secure. When Jesus carved time out of his pressing schedule to spend with children, he was showing us that, truly, the little things are the big things.

It has been said that "the world turns on small hinges." By this, we mean that small, seemingly inconsequential events can sometimes have profound consequences, quite literally changing the world. Open the book of history and here are a few of the pages, now yellowed with age, which might draw your attention …

Notice the hungry boy begging for bread outside the gates of the Andalusia Monastery in Southern Spain. The boy has been left to fend for himself by a wandering father. By coincidence, a priest of that monastery overhears the boy speak of his father. By coincidence, that priest is an old friend of a certain Queen Isabella. He mentions the wandering father to the Queen. In turn, she decides to hire the father to sail one of her ships. The name of that young boy's father? Christopher Columbus. That trip brought Europeans to the New Word. You and I might not be living in America today if, one day long ago, a hungry boy hadn't begged for bread.

Or hear the pounding footsteps! Hear the ragged breath! Fleeing for his life, a man runs into a cave to hide. As it would happen, a busy spider spins down in front of the mouth of that cave just as he passes. In a few moments, his pursuers arrive, bent on killing him. Seeing the spider web across the entrance to the cave, they assume no one has entered for quite some time and they continue their search elsewhere. That man crouched within the darkness of the cave is Robert Bruce, later to be called Robert the First, Father of Scotland. The destiny of millions has just hung upon a single spider web.

Remember also the little boy who shared his lunch with Jesus. One little lad ... one little lunch. Little did he know that his story would be recorded in the pages of the Bible and he would be remembered for centuries to come.

Yes, the gates of history turn on small hinges. In the same way, the gates of Heaven turn on small hinges ...

What is that? He could see it floating in the surf. So he waited and watched. Soon, he saw that it was a handful of pages. He read them, and the Japanese nobleman became so engrossed in the words that he sent for a copy of the entire book. That book was the Bible ... and that is how Christ first came to the Japanese Islands.

Not too far away, inconsolable cries echo through the palace of the Korean queen. Her child has just died. Her grief overwhelms her. But a foreign slave girl says that there is a place called Heaven and there is a Savior who can take her there. And so it is that the Gospel is first brought to Korea ... by a little slave girl.

In another part of the world, drought rages. Famine grips the land. The people of the Telugu region of India turn to Englishman John Cloud because he had once studied some engineering in college. He says he can build a canal that will bring water to the province. And so they call up thousands of workers to begin the task. What they don't know is that John Cloud is a Christian. For the next year, he leads a little devotional service each night after the work is finished. Each and every night, for an entire year, he talks about just one verse in the Bible: "For God so loved the world that He gave His only-begotten Son ...."[15] By the end of the year, Cloud will baptize ten-thousand converts. A single engineer ... given a single year!

Momentous events turn on small hinges. And what do you and I have in common with all these people? *We* are small hinges! The point is, the world – and even eternity itself – is more often changed by a single individual than by a great army. History is often altered by little, apparently insignificant, events.

You may feel small and unimportant. You may feel weak and ineffective. But you are not. You are special. You are unique. There has never been an individual exactly like you and there never will be again. Never again will there exist in this world the same combination of ability, opportunity, and personality as there exists right now wrapped up in you. Therefore, the mark which you make upon this world is matchless. It is unable to be duplicated by anyone else.

Because "the world turns on small hinges," everything you do, every day, matters. Though you may not be able to see the difference you are making, each and every moment of your life is pregnant with eternal possibilities. Each and every moment may be the moment you change history. You may feel like life has knocked you down, but begin each day on fire with this thought: *This day may be the day that will be remembered for all eternity.*

More than that, though the kingdoms, cultures, and corporations of this world will one day pass away, people will not. People are eternal. When you make a mark upon people, it is a mark which will be felt forever. When you alter someone's eternal destiny, you have made a difference that will echo into endless eternity.

My friend, live your life convinced of this thought: *Your efforts will never be forgotten.* Though kingdoms may turn to dust and civilizations may perish, your name will never be forgotten. The mark you make upon others will never be forgotten. In a very real sense, with each little act and effort you make, you scratch your initials into the walls of eternity.

No doubt you've heard of the "Butterfly Effect." Back in the 1960's Dr. Edward Lorenz of M.I.T. performed groundbreaking research in an emerging field known as "Chaos Theory." He discovered in his laboratory that the tiniest variation in weather conditions in one part of the world can produce dramatic changes in weather conditions months later in another part of the world. He argued that, theoretically, a monarch butterfly flapping its wings in Malibu might eventually produce a monsoon in Malaysia.

Do you get the picture? One tiny act can produce profound changes.

Like a butterfly flapping its wings, a simple smile, a friendly wave, a kind word, or a little extra attention given to a child may cause a tsunami of kindness in another corner of the world.

Jesus understood this. It is why he took the time to play with the children on a sunny spring afternoon. It is why he took the time to take them into his arms and bless them. He knew that a little bit of time invested in little ones on a sunny spring day would create a ripple effect that would spread outward through generations to come.

Jesus also knew that time spent with children is the most strategic, for they are the most impressionable. They are the most moldable and malleable. They are the most open to his message.

Have you noticed this as well? Like the potted plant in front of your window that stretches toward the sunlight, children naturally stretch toward the eternal light.

Over the years, I have taught hundreds of little ones the big truths. It is a mysterious thing. Not once has a little one ever argued the existence of God or doubted the love of Jesus. Not once! Instead, when I speak to them about God, they listen to my words as if they are listening to the soft, natural sounds of their native language. When I ask them to fold their hands to pray, they do so naturally, as if I am about to open the door to their homeland, the land for which they have been longing. When I tell them the stories about Jesus and the heroes of the Bible, how their bright eyes shine and their young hearts beat! Never do they argue, "Who is God? I have never seen Him!" Instead they welcome Him. They welcome Him with joy and eagerness, just as the children did that day with Jesus. And the seeds of faith, security, acceptance, and love which we plant now in their young lives will blossom beautifully in the years to come.

Do you remember that sign on my office wall? One hundred years from now the world *will be* different … if you make a difference in the life of a child.

Never forget: The little things are the big things. A simple smile … a little child … a butterfly flapping its wings.

You may feel like nothing you do makes a difference. But you are wrong. This very day is pregnant with potential! This very day may contain that one, tiny, seemingly insignificant event which changes everything. My friend, this could be the day that you will remember for the rest of eternity! For the little things … are the big things.

There is one final lesson I learned that day:
Life may have knocked you down, but …

It's a bounce back world.

The little boy who shared his lunch with Jesus that day reminds me of another little boy I once heard about. Let me tell you about him ...

This poor little fellow was having a very bad day. He followed his mother about the house, moping and complaining. Finally, his mother said, "You need to go outside and get some fresh air! Now, go!"

The little fellow stormed out, slamming the door behind him. He walked to the edge of his yard and then, angry and upset, he shouted at the top of his lungs, "I hate you!"

A second later, a voice shouted back at him, "I hate you!"

The little boy stopped dead in his tracks. What was this? Who would say such a horrible thing to him? Now he shouted all the louder: "You're stupid!"

The voice came back, "You're stupid!"

Angrier than ever, the little boy clenched his fists, drew in a great big breath, and shouted with Herculean might, "Come here and I will fight you!"

Immediately the voice came back, "Come here and I will fight you!"

Frightened now, the little boy ran to his mother's side just as fast as his little legs could carry him. As he explained the whole thing, a wise and knowing look spread over her face.

"Come with me and I will show you something." She took his little hand and walked him back outside. This time, she shouted the words, "I love you!"

Back came the words, "I love you!"

She shouted, "You're terrific!"

Back came the words, "You're terrific!"

The little boy looked up at her with wide eyes. He asked, "Why is he so much nicer to you?"

She said, "Son, that is just something called an 'echo.' Whatever you send out comes bouncing back to you."

Her little boy looked up at her with eyes filled with wonder.

"It is also something called 'life.'"

How true! We live in a bounce back world. *Whatever we send out in life inevitably, invariably, inescapably comes back to us.* Think of the little boy who offered his meager lunch – five little loaves and two dried fish – to Jesus. Everything that little boy gave to Jesus soon came back to him, as surely as an echo rolls back across the hills.

This is a principle that is always in operation. It is a law of life as surely as gravity is a law of physics. And it is a law that is always in operation. You can see this, can't you? When you give someone a smile, they return your smile. When you give someone your friendship, they respond with friendship. And when you give generously, you will receive generously.

So, the question, then, is this: What have you been sending out into this world lately? Have you been positive and generous? Have you been encouraging? Or have you been negative, bitter, and tightfisted? Too often, in discouraging times, we grow cynical and guarded. We close ourselves off from others and want to cling fiercely to the little we have. But this is a mistake. Just the opposite must occur. We must learn to give – and give generously. We must be bighearted and openhanded. We must be unsparing with our encouragement, our affection, and our resources. For here is the simple truth: It is a bounce back world. It is an echo earth. Whatever we send out in life inevitably, invariably, inescapably comes back to us.

But there is more to this universal principle. Not only does your gift return to you, it returns in *multiplied form.* Jesus put it this way: "Give and it shall be given to you. If you give, you will receive. Your gift will return to you in full measure, pressed down, shaken together to make room for more, and running over." He added, "Whatever measure you use in giving – large or small – will be used to measure what is given back to you!"[16]

The image Jesus used here is an image I am familiar with from the days I spent in Galilee, at Jesus' side. Often I saw the laborers in the fields. It was a common sight. Once, when it was spring time, the time of planting, Jesus explained the practice of the Galilean people to me as we walked along the country roads.

He pointed to one busy farmer, tossing handfuls of seed from the rugged cloth sling tied about his waist. "You see this?" he said. "The farmers will sow their seed in the springtime. Then they will labor over their fields, cultivating and caring for them in the months to come. In the fall, these same fields will be overflowing, rich with the harvest."

Jesus continued to explain the unique customs to me: "When harvest time arrives, the entire field will be ready for harvest at once, and they will need to bring in the entire crop as soon as possible. Therefore, the landowner will hire day laborers to help bring in the harvest. These laborers are typically paid by the basket. The more baskets they gather, the more pay they will receive. If they are good workers, the landowner is likely to give them a bonus at the end of the day. He will permit them to pick one last basket and keep it for themselves."

Now the storyteller in Jesus is beginning to kick in. His voice grows more animated. His gestures grow larger. "So, Jeff, imagine the change that falls over that worker! Imagine the change in motivation! All through the day, that worker has been trying to fill a basket as quickly as possible and carry it quickly to the tallyman to get it recorded on the tally sheet. All through the day, he tries to keep each basket light and easy to carry." Jesus breaks into a broad smile. "But now this last basket is for *himself*! It is for *his own family!* Think of the difference! Now, as he gathers this last basket of grain, he is sure to get the full measure. He fills his basket right to the top. He then shakes it, settling the grain, making room for more. Even when the grain is cascading over the brim, he pushes it down with both hands to make room for as much as possible."

"This," explains Jesus, "is how our Father gives to us." There is joy in Jesus' voice, such joy. There is excitement. "Not only does everything we give come back to us, it comes back in multiplied form. Our Father takes the measure we use – whether the tiniest thimble or the deepest basket – and He uses this as the bucket to give back to us. Then He jams and crams the bucket full, pressing it down, shaking it together, and spilling it over into our lap!"

With his explanation complete, Jesus playfully pushes me, slapping my shoulder good-naturedly. I wished all could see it as clearly and simply as he explained it.

Yes, we truly live in a bounce back world. What we give comes bouncing back to us. Moreover it comes bouncing back in multiplied form.

Now, here is the practical thing about this law of life. Here is the powerful thing. This means … *You get to decide the level of blessing in your life.* You get to decide … because you get to decide what to give. You get to decide the measure you will use. Because all of this depends upon you taking the first step, you yourself decide the level of bounty and blessing which you will experience in life.

However, there is a frightening part to this law of life. It takes faith. It takes faith for the farmer to throw good seed out onto the barren earth each spring. It takes faith for a little boy to give away his lunch. Think of it! That little boy who gave away his five loaves and two fish could not possibly see how he would ever get them back. I'm certain he believed he would go to bed with an empty stomach that night. And, in fact, he might have. Though we are told that our gift will return to us in full and overflowing measure, we are not told *when.* Therefore it is a risk. That is why Jesus likened our giving to planting a seed and waiting for an eventual harvest, rather than putting coins in a vending machine and expecting an immediate return. Yet, plant a seed we must. We can't hope for a harvest if we haven't planted the seed.

I, for one, am in the planting stage right now. I have given. I have sacrificed. I have supported our ministry from my own pocket. Kathy and I have drained our savings and emptied our checking accounts to plant a worthy crop. But now we are in the waiting stage. How long until the harvest? How long until one season turns to the next? How long?

Only this I know: It is a bounce back world. It is an echo earth. Give and it shall be given. If you want to experience a new level of blessing, you have a decision to make. If you have a need, plant a seed. If you are waiting to see the blessing and bounty of God, hang in there. Trust Him. Just as surely as one season rolls around after another, your blessing is rolling your way.

Key Discovery
It's a bounce back world.

Part Four

Entry 12
A Mountain View

Thursday, October 20, 2:09 p.m. ...

I'm at my desk, an array of financial reports spread out in front of me. I'm scanning profit and loss reports, past due amounts, future projections. I'm making notes on a legal pad, preparing. I have a telephone conference with our primary lender, the Minneapolis-based bank which holds our mortgage, scheduled for 3:00. Less than an hour away. Less than an hour before I know what decisions they will make about our future. I'm trying to anticipate their questions, reviewing my presentation.

2:19 p.m. ...

I tear my reading glasses off and throw them down on top of the papers which litter my desk. Then I push away from the desk and begin to pace back and forth, filled with nervous energy.

Nine steps forward. Turn. Nine steps backward. It seems to be the story of my life. Nine steps forward. Turn. Nine steps backward. Never any real progress.

When the bank officers call from Minneapolis, I will attempt to explain why we have not sent them a cent in four months. I will attempt to convince them that we are still a good bet for the future, that if they simply give us more time, we will turn this around. But, as I review the numbers in my head, I know what they will be thinking: Nine steps forward. Turn. Nine steps backward. Never any real progress. That's what they will be thinking.

2:29 p.m. …
A half-hour, give or take, until the conference call. I decide to grab a coffee. Maybe the caffeine will sharpen my thinking. I hurriedly swing open my office door, charge out into the corridor, and pass quickly by the other offices without pausing to speak to anyone. As I push open the next door, to step from the office corridor into the lobby, I am ready for the lobby's soothing piped-in music, the flashing flatscreen advertising our upcoming events, and the sounds of children laughing from the classrooms, but …

I am on the top of a mountain.
The air is thin. A stiff breeze snaps at my robe. The sunlight has a silvery, white quality to it. I can see for miles, as I gaze out over the rich, flat valley far below. I see a breathtaking panorama of distant green meadows, golden fields of wheat, and tiny white-washed stone villages.
I hear footsteps on the gravel behind me and whip around, startled. A moment later I'm being crushed in the great, big, bear hug of Peter! John and James, their faces lit up with animated smiles, slap me on the back. "It's good to see you!" they exclaim. "This is the last place we would expect to run into you!"
I grin from ear to ear, overjoyed to see my friends. As Peter releases me from his thick, burly arms, Jesus takes his turn. He throws his arms tightly around me, pounding my back with his fist a couple of times for good measure. My whole world lights up when I see Jesus, with fireworks of joy bursting deep inside and spreading outward, the joy rising all the way to my face, which explodes with easy laughter.
After the usual friendly banter, my curiosity takes over. "Why are we here? On top of this mountain?" I ask.
Jesus explains that he has a meeting scheduled – some sort of important conference. *So, I'm not the only one who has a conference scheduled for this afternoon.*

"And you need *me* to be at this meeting?" I inquire.

"Not exactly," Jesus answers. "Let's just say I like the company. Remember, Jeff, I told you I see something special in you." There go the fireworks inside of me again, a fresh volley exploding!

"Plus, I have something I want to show you."

Turning to the others, Jesus says: "Have a seat. We're going to be here awhile."

Jesus walks on a bit further, about a stone's throw away. Then he turns away from us, toward the great open expanse of air that stretches before us and the vast valley that stretches below us. With eyes open, he begins to speak. He speaks in a casual, conversational tone. Soon, his words become more intense, his gestures more animated. He raises his hands to the level of his waist and turns his palms upward. "Abba…"

The pale sun inches slowly through the cloudless sky. Jesus sits on a stony seat, carved ages ago by the hand of nature on the crest of this rocky shelf. He prays quietly. Occasionally his lips move, a silent sentence escaping. This continues for some time, how long I cannot say. Peter, James, and John, their bodies worn and their muscles weary from the long climb, grow drowsy in the afternoon sun. I see their eyes grow heavy, blinking back sleep.

All at once, something is happening – something which cannot be put into words. I can say only this: Like a thick curtain being torn back in one sudden thrust, a burst of blazing light floods the mountaintop. The world is washed with light, drowns in light, flows with light. The light comes not from the sun above, it comes from Jesus. His appearance is changing from the inside out, right before our very eyes. We are witnessing a metamorphosis. His face shines with the light of a thousand suns. His clothing is dazzling white.

Now we are wide-awake, all of us, gaping with once-sleepy eyes at this once-plain carpenter. I fall to my knees, but cannot look away.

Jesus stands up abruptly, stepping forward eagerly as if he is ready to welcome a friend to his home. Suddenly – inexplicably – there are two men standing with him. Both shine as bright as lightening. Both wear robes which appear to be woven of pure sunlight. Like Jesus, they glisten with glory and shimmer like sunshine flashing on water.

One is Moses. He steps forward forcefully, clasping arms with Jesus. I look at him in wonder. Here is the great hero of the Bible, who knew firsthand the glory of Egypt and who walked the marbled courts of Pharaoh's palace. Moses, who led the nation of Israel out of slavery and delivered them to the doorstep of the Promised Land. Moses, who received the Ten Commandments carved upon tablets of stone by the very finger of God. He stands before us, just a stone's throw away, speaking earnestly with Jesus about the critical importance of the next few months.

The other is Elijah, greatest of the Old Testament prophets. Elijah has seen great miracles and experienced great triumphs. But Elijah has also known great depression and defeat. He knows firsthand what it feels like when all the odds are stacked against you, when the obstacles in your path are insurmountable, and when even those you thought you could trust turn against you. According to the Bible, Elijah was last seen being swept up into the heavens in a chariot of fire. But now I see him. I see him standing before me, speaking quietly with Jesus.

How do I know it is, in fact, Moses and Elijah who stand before me? There is no mistaking it. I know from the conversation which takes place. I know as they review the precise details of the plan which must fall into place in the weeks ahead. Moses speaks openly to Jesus about his impending death – he calls it his "exodus," his departure, which will soon take place in Jerusalem.[17] Elijah acknowledges that, if everything goes precisely as planned, Jesus will fulfill every word ever prophesied about God's Promised Savior. This will prove to the people, who know well the teachings of the prophets, that Jesus is indeed the very one for whom they have waited for so many centuries.

Suddenly, I see the whole grand sweep of Scripture standing before me, embodied in these men, captured in this moment. Moses, bearer of the Ten Commandments, personifies the timeless Law of God. Elijah, foremost of God's spokesmen, embodies the Prophets of God. These two represent God's Old Covenant, God's old agreement with humankind. But Jesus ... Jesus represents the new. I look on, caught up, marveling at this moment. The Old Covenant of the Law and Prophets now stands face to face with the New Covenant.

Here, on this glory-washed mountaintop, the Old and the New clasp hands.

Peter immediately reacts. He is a man of action. Leave it to Peter to be direct. While the rest of us are too stunned to speak, Peter blurts out: "This is amazing! This is wonderful! This is...." Peter cannot find any more words. He naturally falls into his role of being Jesus' trusted lieutenant, ready to organize a practical response to this unheard of situation. "It is good for us to be here!"

Peter exclaims. "I will build three shelters – one for you, one for Moses, and one for Elijah."

Suddenly, before Jesus even has a chance to respond to Peter, a great cloud sweeps over us. It comes quickly, overshadowing us completely, layering us in thick, warm, softness. The cloud is brilliant, with a quality of glory unlike anything we have yet seen. It is bright, like a beneficent presence; not dark, as if to threaten.

The cloud envelopes me completely, hugging me in warmth. I am now wrapped in a soft blanket. My heart is pounding. I feel only one thing: pure and perfect love.

Then, in the moments that follow, a rainbow of emotions flow rapidly through me, one after the other. I feel a sense of complete and utter well-being, though just a short time earlier I had been overwrought with anxiety as I anticipated my upcoming telephone conference. I feel no trace of fear, though the cloud completely overshadows me. I feel like I belong. Yes, I belong here more than I have ever belonged anywhere in my life. I feel goodness. Pure and undiluted goodness.

And, hardest to explain, I feel like myself. Yes, at this moment, I feel more truly myself than ever before. Indeed, as the cloud swirls around me, I see most clearly. I see my life, its whole spectrum and span. I see my worth, abilities, and gifts. I see that I am more valuable than I have ever imagined. And, though this sounds odd, I see that I am more beautiful than I ever conceived.

I feel this all, all in these few moments within the white-bright cloud of glory. I hold these thoughts in my head for only a few fragile moments, balanced precariously in my consciousness. I will be able to recall only fragments of this later. This self-image will fall away the moment the cloud lifts, shattering like a mirror that is dropped. But at this moment I see it – I see it all – all that I am, all that I was created to become.

Suddenly a voice rumbles out of the cloud, a voice that echoes like thunder from deep, deep within me. "This is My Son ... and I love Him!" They are the affectionate words of a proud father. I watch Jesus smile. It is a great, broad smile that swells up from deep within, as the great love of the Father rests upon him.

Instantly, the thick curtain is pulled back, shutting out our glimpse of glory. The mountaintop that radiated with light now rests in shadows. The bright cloud has lifted. It is gone.

The sun-splashed mountaintop now appears gray and lackluster. It is without dimension. It is entirely dreary. The world now looks like an artist's watercolor that has had too much water spilled over it. It is washed out. It is faded. The remnants of the landscape are still there, yet it all looks quite pale and lifeless.

We are alone. Only Jesus remains with us, a quite average looking Jesus. The Prince of Heaven, who moments ago blazed with glory, now appears to be but a mundane Galilean carpenter, with calloused hands and dusty feet.

He steps up to me, rests a hand on my shoulder, and simply states, "I wanted to share that with you."[18]

Later, as we're hiking down the winding, rock-strewn path from the summit, Jesus speaks to us about the great plan that was long ago set into motion. "My Father and I are going to retake this world," explains Jesus resolutely. "The campaign is already underway."

Jesus looks from one to another of us, his face set like stone. "But for this plan to work, I must suffer many things. Be ready for bloodshed and betrayal. Be ready to have your heart broken. That's why I wanted to share this day with you. When your world gets incredibly dark, I want you to know that there is glory waiting for you on the other side."

We are silent for a long time, not knowing what to say. Then Jesus speaks again, breaking the silence. "Don't tell anyone what you have seen today until after I have risen from the dead."

Peter's brow furrows with confusion. "What does he mean by 'risen from the dead'?" Peter looks over to John, who only shrugs. Later that day – and often in the days to come – we will ask each other, "'Risen from the dead?' What can he mean by that?"[19]

I should have known. But I didn't. I was blind – utterly blind to where events were leading. Wrapped in the fog of the First Century, I could not see. I could not see what was waiting for us in Jerusalem. But I could sense it. Another Passover is fast approaching. And death is drawing near. Silent and stalking, it is creeping closer. And it scares me. I am now confident of the glory. But I am *not* confident I will have the strength to make it through the darkness.

Entry 13
A Frantic Father

It is late afternoon. The descent took the better part of a day. We are to meet up with the other disciples in a village not far from Caesarea Philippi, a small, sleepy farm village that looks little changed since the days of David.

But as we approach the village we see that it has been invaded by an uncountable hoard of people, a multitude which covers the terrain like a swarm of locust. People from all over the Galilean territories have followed Jesus to this remote location. They search for him throughout the village and in every quiet corner and hidden hamlet in the region. Now seeing his approach, they begin to converge on him from every direction, running to him, pushing others, wanting to see him, touch him, hear him. An electricity fills the air.

People are yelling. People are pressing in tightly. Someone calls out: "Jesus! Teacher! Please!" The man waves his hand in the air, trying to distinguish himself from the throng.

Jesus directs his attention to the man.

"Teacher, I brought my son in order for you to heal him. He can't speak because he is possessed by an evil spirit that won't let him talk. And whenever this evil spirit seizes him, it throws him violently to the ground and it makes him foam at the mouth and grind his teeth and become as stiff as a board. I asked your disciples to cast out the evil spirit – but they couldn't do it!"

Jesus exhales a long, exasperated sigh. There is pain and disappointment in the tone of his voice: "Bring the boy to me."

The crowd parts and a thin, timid, little boy is pushed toward the front. He is perhaps eight or nine years old. He looks no different than any little boy in this village.

The crowd falls silent, eager to see what will happen next. The boy steps out from the crowd. He looks shy and uncertain. His little sandals slap the sandy road as he walks forward.

His deep brown eyes look up into the eyes of Jesus.

Suddenly, as if hurled to the ground by an unseen force, he is thrown into a violent seizure. He falls face forward, writhing and foaming at the mouth. He convulses brutally, as if a demon has indeed become enraged and is venting its horrible power upon him.

The father races forward, falls to his knees, and takes the boy into his arms, trying to restrain him and keep him from further injury.

As the seizure begins to release its iron grip and the boy's rigid body begins to relax, Jesus shakes his head sadly.

"How long has he been like this?" he asks the father.

"Ever since he was a little boy," the father answers. "Many times the evil spirit throws him into a fire or into the water, trying to kill him."

The father looks directly into the eyes of Jesus, pleading. "Have mercy on us. Help us. Please. Do something if you can."

"What do you mean, *'If I can'*?" Jesus replies. "All things are possible if a person believes."

Instantly the father pleads, "I do believe – but help me overcome my doubts!"

Now there are tears in the eyes of the father. Now there is hope spilling over. Now there is intense emotion pouring into every syllable of his words.

Jesus stares directly into the deep brown eyes of the little boy. Then, in a voice that rumbles like a sudden clap of thunder, he gives the order. "You spirit that robs this boy of his hearing and speech, I command you to get out of this child and never enter him again!"

No sooner do the words fly from his mouth, than the demon screams an inhuman shriek, the sound of a dying animal. The crowd backs away in fear. The scream contains all the demon's rage at being forced to abandon its victim. The boy convulses violently – but this will be the last vicious damage the demon can inflict upon him.

Then it's gone.

It disappears as abruptly as a candle being blown out. And, like a wisp of smoke that dissipates into the night, it is gone forever.

The moment the demon leaves, the boy's body relaxes. He lies in the dirt, empty and spent. He is as pale and as motionless as a corpse. His father reaches down to lift his crumpled body.

"He's dead," murmurs one man.

"It's over," says another.

They shake their heads sadly, as the news spreads through the crowd.

Jesus does not correct them. In fact, he does not even look at them. He simply goes to the boy and kneels beside him. Quietly, he takes his pale, little hand. Without saying a single word, he gives the hand a tug. And ...

The boy stands up.

A gasp rolls through the crowd.

Jesus speaks tenderly to the overwrought father. "I have a gift for you," he says with a smile.

"Dad ... here is your son."[20]

Entry 14
A Troubling Tax

Within the week, we are back in Capernaum. It feels good to be home. Capernaum has been our base of operations for the past three years. Peter's family is here; Jesus feels at home here.[21] But the visit is brief. It will be the very last time Jesus visits his own city.

Peter and I are walking through the narrow streets near the waterfront. Shopkeepers hawk their wares, men barter heatedly, women make their careful selections for the evening meal. The air is full of the smell of bread baking, butchered meat, and fresh fish from the day's catch.

As we near the heart of the market area, two officials from the synagogue approach us. As they make their way in our direction, Peter leans in close to me and speaks quietly under his breath. "I know these two. And they're up to no good."

"How do you know them?" I ask.

"They're the ones who collect the Annual Temple Tax."

Every man in Israel must pay an annual tax to be used for the upkeep of the Temple. Sensing my confusion, Peter explains: "Since we have been traveling so much, I suspect we have not paid for this year yet. It doesn't surprise me that they would want to approach me in the middle of the marketplace about it. They won't miss a chance to embarrass me."

As Peter spits out the words, the two officials reach us. In an authoritative voice, the taller of the two loudly questions, "Doesn't your teacher pay the Temple Tax?"

A vendor from the cart next to us looks up. A woman stops her shopping and turns to listen to the exchange.

Getting a bit hot under the collar, Peter replies, "Of course he does."

I can see the color beginning to rise to Peter's face.

"Well, *words* will not support our Temple," fires back the official. "Let us see the *coin*."

Peter abruptly turns his back on the officials and storms off, leaving me to push through the busy marketplace to catch up.

Peter heads straightaway to the home where Jesus is staying. As he bursts through the door, still red-faced and sputtering, Jesus is the first to speak.

"So, what do you think, Peter?"

"What?" Peter is caught up short. He has come with a particular agenda in mind, but Jesus has seized control by speaking first.

"I said, what do you think?" Jesus repeats.

"About what?" Peter replies, with no small measure of exasperation.

Jesus continues, his eyes wide, his tone playful. "From whom do the kings of this earth collect tribute and taxes – from their own sons or from others?"

"From others," answers Peter, still unsure where this line of discussion is leading.

"Exactly!" replies Jesus, clapping his hands together lightly. "The king does not demand taxes from his own children. Instead, the entire royal family is supported in regal fashion by taxing the people. A king collects taxes only from outsiders, not from the princes of the royal house."

A smile begins to spread over Peter's face. The implication is clear. Jesus is royalty! He is the Prince of Heaven! He and his disciples belong to the royal household of God and therefore, one could reason, are exempt from paying a Temple Tax!

Yet, before Peter can run too far with this thought, Jesus continues. "But, so that we do not upset them needlessly, here is what I want you to do. Go down to the waterfront and throw out a fishing line. Then pull in the first fish that bites. Open its mouth and you will find a coin. Take that coin, Peter – and pay the tax for both of us!"

Peter's face lights up! He nods his head excitedly, then wheels around and heads out. I call after him, "I'll catch up with you in just a minute."[22]

Turning to Jesus, I can stand it no more. "Lord, can I talk to you for a minute?"

"Of course," answers Jesus. "Always."

"Lord, I have seen so many things. I have watched you feed thousands from a few loaves and fish. I have seen your glory and your power. And I have seen your love. And now I even see you take care of a small thing, one mere coin for a minor tax."

Jesus nods, understanding.

"But, Lord, I am about to lose everything. Certainly you know what I am going through back at home. I pray, and I plead, and I pour out my heart to you, yet you do nothing. I was literally just minutes away from meeting with bank officials. Minutes! Will you make me lose everything I have worked for?"

Jesus still remains silent.

"Lord, you care about little things … like a single little coin. Why don't you care about me?"

Now he speaks.

"Jeff, I do care. More than you know."

Now I am the silent one. I don't even know where to go with this.

"Jeff, why do you assume that I will only act as you would expect? Certainly if there is anything you have seen in your time with me it is that I seldom act as others expect. Think of what I just told Peter to do. Would you have guessed that I would provide for that need by having Peter discover a coin in the mouth of a *fish?*"

"I'm sorry, Lord, but none of this makes any sense to me."

"Jeff, you've read the words of Scripture: 'As high as the heavens are above the earth, so high are My ways above your ways, and My thoughts above your thoughts.'[23] Not to insult you, Jeff, but my Father and I are operating on a whole different level than anything you can even begin to wrap your mind around."

Jesus pauses to give my mind time to catch up. Then he continues with a friendly laugh. "In fact, if you could understand all that we are doing, Jeff, that would be pretty scary! Don't you think? That would mean that we are no smarter than you!"

I am forced to chuckle at that. I can't help myself.

"Jeff, you're a dad. When your children were small, were there times when you were forced to make a decision that your children could not understand?"

"Of course."

"For example, I suppose your children would prefer to eat ice cream sundaes every night for dinner, rather than a healthy meal. Perhaps they would even beg and plead for those ice cream sundaes."

"Yes," I reply, "That sounds like my kids."

"So, at times you had to say no to them. You had to say no, even though they hungered for it and wanted it with all their heart … even though they were convinced that they knew what was best … even though you seemed hard and uncaring when you denied them."

I stare blankly into the eyes of Jesus, my heart suddenly pounding hard in my chest. "Are you trying to tell me that you are going to say no to me and deny me the help I've been praying for?"

"No, Jeff, what I am trying to tell you is that you have to trust me."

I'm not sure this makes me feel any better.

"Just as you had to decide what was best for your children, my Father must decide what is best for His. Your children could not begin to understand the complexities of your decisions – what food is healthy, what bedtime is best, a thousand other things. And you cannot begin to understand the decisions my Father will make. Just remember this: We see something very special in you."

I draw in a deep breath and release it slowly.

Jesus places a hand on my shoulder and smiles encouragingly.

"All things are possible with God, Jeff. Just believe!"

A short time later, I catch up with Peter. He is down at the wharf, already aboard one of his boats, leaning precariously over the stern with a single fishing line in hand. He tosses the line into the clear, sunlit waters below. Brown shadows dart back and forth beneath the boat.

Immediately there is tug on the line. Peter quickly jerks the line upward, pulling in the dripping cord, coiling it expertly at his feet. He has hooked a strong, young carp, its silver scales shimmering, its gills heaving. As Peter removes the hook from its mouth, the fish kicks angrily.

"Hold on there, fella."

He sticks a prodding finger into its gasping mouth.

"Yes, I feel something in there."

Peter pulls something wet and warm and shiny from the mouth of the fish.

Then, though the young carp is a good-sized fish and could bring Peter some decent money in the marketplace, Peter gently places it back into the sea. With a swift flick of its tail, it slides silently through the sunlit waters and disappears from sight.

Peter holds out his hand to show me.

It is a coin.

It is the exact amount needed to pay the Temple Tax for Peter and for Jesus. We both laugh at the wonder of it all.

And then I remember his words to me.

"All things are possible with God."

All things indeed.

Entry 15
A Difficult Meeting

Inhale ...

Exhale ...

Inhale ...

Exhale ...

Inhale ... I breathe in the briny air of the sea. Gulls circle above and cry out hungrily. Waves lap gently against the hull of the wooden boat.

Exhale ... I breathe out – and I step out – into the lobby.

I stumble, mid-stride, through the office corridor door, trying to regain my equilibrium. Restoring my stride is not difficult. Restoring my inner orientation – not so easy.

I have lived for nine days – in the past second. Nine days – in the split-second flash between placing my hand upon the door and pushing the door open.

My mind cannot comprehend a change so drastic, so dramatic, which can happen in a single breath.

Inhale …

Exhale…

The whole thing is, literally, breathtaking.

I continue on for the coffee which I planned so long ago. I continue, if for no other reason than to simply give my head a chance to clear.

My telephone conference is a disaster. I intend to walk them through the numbers, but immediately they wrestle control of the agenda from me. They speak of the need for considering all options. They remind me of the responsibility they have to their investors. They address the probability of taking drastic action, such as dividing and selling off our land or separating the various business entities which operate under the umbrella of the church and selling them each off separately. I am tasked with meeting with local realtors to gain an appraisal of the current market value of our property and its various pieces. I am required to conference with them again in exactly two weeks.

When I hang up the phone, I am at least grateful that immediate foreclosure did not enter the conversation. This, I suppose, is a victory of sorts. I have been given two weeks … a stay of execution.

One minute after the conference call ends, Kathy bursts into my office. She is holding a piece of paper. It's a bill. "The repairman just handed me this," she states, her face exasperated. She is referring to the repairman who had to be called to address a non-functioning freezer at our restaurant. "This is his bill for the work he did on the freezer unit. He's charging us $900 for labor – and, get this! He didn't even fix the problem! He still needs to order a part."

I'm struck by the tremendous disconnect between my life here, where I'm treading water, trying to stay afloat, and not doing too good of a job of it at that, and my life in Galilee, where even trifling taxes are immediately, miraculously taken care of.

What did I discover on this past trip? What was I permitted to see and experience – and why? I need to record it, put it all on paper, sort it out, while it is still fresh in my mind. I think somewhere in those experiences will be the answer to my worries, my fears, and my discouragement. I have been pessimistic, but that needs to change.

The first big truth that hits me, as I scan the experiences of the past nine days, is this …

God has a plan … and it is good.

High on a Galilean mountain, I caught a glimpse of glory. I saw Jesus blaze with the light of another world.

But, more than that, I saw him meet with Moses and Elijah. There they spoke of a plan that transcended the centuries. Moses spoke to Jesus about how the time had come to deliver people from their captivity to sin and death, just as he, Moses, had once delivered people from their captivity in Egypt. He spoke of the precise timing of Jesus' "exodus," meaning his departure from this world, his death. It would occur at the Passover, on the exact anniversary of Moses' departure from Egypt. Elijah noted how all this was unfolding according to a precise plan, fulfilling the ancient words of the prophets. Truly, this was a plan that scanned the entire timeline of human history. It had been set into action centuries earlier.

Perhaps you feel like your life is difficult and confusing. You can't understand why things are happening as they are. Like me, you're struggling. *The good news is, you are a part of this plan.* Like Moses and Elijah, you have a part to play. God has chosen a role for you. He has placed you in this generation, in this moment, in this situation, to play that role. And He has equipped you with everything you need to be successful in that role.

Never before in the long course of human history has there existed the exact intersection of ability, opportunity, and personality that now exists in you. Never.

Why, then, do we allow ourselves to become so pessimistic? Why do we mope along through the day as if the sky is about to fall upon us? No, look up! The truth is, the sky isn't falling – that's just the heavens opening up!

Suddenly, I experience a breakthrough. I see things in an entirely different light. I see things, even if just for a moment, as they really are. I am a part of God's plan. I am not trapped in a cycle of random events. I have been chosen and equipped for this moment. I have been given everything I need in order to accomplish what God calls me to do. Rather than being a *pessimist*, I should instead in every way be the ultimate *optimist!*

This is a complete shift in perspective, a metamorphosis as dramatic as anything I witnessed on that mountaintop. I have been focused on my problems. But, all at once, my entire worldview alters – from dark to light. Suddenly, I see it! Here is the breakthrough that comes to me in that instant:

I have every right to declare myself "The Ultimate Optimist."

And so do you.

Yes, it's absolutely true! From this point on, that is what I am: "The Ultimate Optimist."

Why? Because I know that, *ultimately, everything will work to my advantage.* Everything. I take this assurance from the most positive book ever written: the Bible. Here is what the Bible says, "All things work together for good for those who love God."[24] Yes, that's it. Read those words more slowly. "All things." Yes, that means even the difficulties you and I are now experiencing. "Work together." Nothing is random. Nothing falls to chance or slips through the cracks. Everything fits into the plan. "For good." The whole universe runs on a positive wavelength. Even the problem you currently struggle with will one day prove to work to your advantage.

It's no wonder I am The Ultimate Optimist! The Bible says, "Surely goodness and love will follow me all the days of my life, and I will dwell in the house of the Lord forever."[25] The original Hebrew word which is translated as "follow" can also mean "to chase after," "to pursue," "to hunt down." In other words, good things, good breaks, and good blessings are pursuing me every hour of every day! And good things are pursuing *you!* Maybe all the blessings God has arranged for you have not yet caught up to you, that is true. But just wait! They are right on your heels. They are just around the corner, not yet in sight. They are hunting you down and will surely overtake you. Good things are coming your way.

I am The Ultimate Optimist because I am supremely confident that, ultimately, inevitably, good things will catch up to me. Even if I now walk through a dark valley, even if the days are long and the difficulties many, even if dark death itself finds me, I will dwell in the house of the Lord forever. One day the curtain will be pulled back once and for all, and the glory I glimpsed on that mountaintop will be mine forever.

"But, Jeff," you say to me with some measure of doubt. "What about all the times I've made bad decisions? The times I have been selfish and sinful? The times I have been hurt and wronged by others? Can all of that be a part of God's plan?"

Friend, God can even take the bad times and fit them into His good plan. Think of it this way … Have you ever tried to make chocolate chip cookies? I have, with my children. You take two or three cups of flour, a teaspoon or two of baking soda, a couple of sticks of butter, some raw eggs and all sorts of other things. You mix it all up in a big bowl. The result, with any luck, is something that makes your mouth water just thinking about it!

But consider each of these ingredients. Taken individually, by themselves, many of them are quite distasteful. Raw eggs? Baking soda? Try swallowing down a heaping spoonful of raw flour! It's only when these ingredients are mixed together that something delicious is created.

In the same way, many of the things that we experience in life are quite distasteful. We experience things that are hard to stomach. But our Father is so good to us, He is able to mix all the ingredients in our life together and produce something wonderful!

In fact, many of life's most dark and distasteful experiences will one day serve to wonderfully highlight the glory we will experience on a daily basis when we at last "dwell in the house of the Lord forever."

Again, think of it this way … Have you ever been in a building that towers several stories? Near my home is a large mall with shopping on several levels. As I walk along the ground level, I may notice that the floor has several colors of tile. Some are white and off-white. Others are nearly black. As I walk around peering in the store windows, there is no clearly distinguishable pattern to the tile design. It's only when I ride the escalator to the floor above, and peer down over the side of the balcony, that I can see a beautiful pattern to the tiled floors below. Now I see beautiful symmetry, great sweeps of curve and color, and careful design.

In the same way, you're going to go through some bright, beautiful times in life, and you're going to go through some pretty dark times. You won't understand it all when you're going through it. You may be in a dark time right now and you're thinking, *Why am I going through this? God, why don't you answer my prayers?* But one day, from up above, when you're in heaven, you'll look at your life and see how God arranged everything in a perfect pattern. You'll see that there was a beautiful design to your life. From heaven's vantage point, we will see the great sweep of history, the careful design of our Creator, and the intricate plan and pattern. Moreover, you will one day see that even the dark times served a purpose. They, too, fit into the plan.

You say, "But, how can I feel optimistic? Right now I just feel broken. All my plans are wrecked. All my dreams are shattered."

The story is told of an architect who ordered large, exquisite mirrors to be shipped from Paris to be used in the decoration of the Royal Palace in Tehran. However, when the mirrors arrived, it was discovered that the entire order had shattered during shipment. The great wooden crates contained only broken shards and sharp fragments. The contractor was furious and quickly made arrangements to dispose of the broken pieces. But, when the architect heard of the dilemma, he had a brilliant idea! He used the broken shards to create a magnificent mosaic of glittering glass, which covered the walls of the palace in a spectacular design. When the royal family finally entered the palace to see the finished results, they saw the light of a thousand diamonds reflecting back at them from every direction. The entire room glittered. The effect was breathtaking.

In the same way, God can take all the broken pieces of our life and fit them together into a beautiful mosaic which will reflect His glory for all eternity. God certainly doesn't bring the bad into our lives. He doesn't turn a blind eye to our mistakes. Nor does He think the dark times through which we pass are a small matter. However, He can take whatever we give Him and He can turn it into something beautiful.

Yes, God has a plan. It is a big plan. It is a good plan. And you and I are a part of it. Even our dark times, difficulties, and brokenness can be fitted into it.

That's why I'm …

The Ultimate Optimist!

The second thing that struck me after spending nine days with Jesus is …

The road is rough … but don't give up.

I'm an optimist. But I'm also a realist.

Like Peter, I longed to spend more time on that mountaintop. Peter's first response was to build shelters and camp out for awhile. Mine was, *Pete, build one for me, too. I want to stay!* There on that mountaintop I glimpsed the glory. I was hugged in the warmth of my Father's presence. I rubbed shoulders with heroes. Why would I ever want to leave? There was no difficulty, no stress, no conflict.

Yet, the mountaintop experience was short lived. Soon we were trudging down the rocky path, reentering everyday life. And what did we find? Immediately we were submerged into the chaos of needy people, difficulty, and pessimism.

Do you recall what we encountered the minute we hit the bottom of the mountain? We encountered a frantic father and a tormented boy – and a group of disciples who were ineffective in following through on even the simplest ministry plan. It was a scene characterized by complete frustration, disappointment, and discouragement.

Even days later, when we finally made it back to Capernaum, we were immediately confronted with the issue of the payment of the Annual Temple Tax. Now, think of this. Capernaum was our home. It's where Peter ran his business and lived his entire life; it's where Jesus based himself during his years of public ministry. This was home – the place where we should be loved, welcomed, and accepted; the place where we should be able to relax and get away from it all. But even in our own home, we were subject to conflict, tax issues, and petty "people" problems.

Yes, the road is rough. Most of life is spent in the valley, not on the mountaintop. We face plenty of obstacles each day. But don't give up! Instead, look up! There is a God in heaven who is one-hundred percent on your side. And here is the good news: *You plus God are bigger than any obstacle.* Therefore, that problem you are facing right now is nothing more than an "obstacle illusion."

You've heard of "optical" illusions, right? An optical illusion is something that isn't really what it appears to be. For example, if you stand on railroad tracks and look down those tracks as far as you can see toward the horizon, what do your eyes tell you the tracks are doing? Your eyes tell you those tracks are getting closer and closer together, until they finally converge. But if you walk down that track, would you ever find a point where they actually converge? No. (If they do, it's time to get off the train!) But, no, it's an optical illusion. What you see doesn't equal what is real.

In the same way, you may be staring at some obstacle in your life, some difficulty, and you're thinking, *I can never get past that. I might as well give up.* But that's an illusion – because you plus God are bigger than any obstacle.

What "obstacle illusions" are holding you down? What is it for you? Maybe you hate your job, but you don't even look for another, because you keep telling yourself you'll never get a good job; you've gone as far as you can go with your qualifications. Maybe you're single and you're telling yourself you'll never meet the right person, the one person you can spend your life with. Maybe you've had some bad breaks and you've given up, you've settled, because you're convinced you just have bad luck and it's too hard to change. My friends, those are "obstacle illusions."

Don't let "obstacle illusions" hold you down.

You can be like a young woman I heard about. When Phyllis was a sixteen-year-old, she got pregnant and dropped out of high school. She rented a small, shabby apartment and went on welfare. Month after month, she barely got by.

Eventually Phyllis got a job working at a school cafeteria collecting meal tickets. The job only paid minimum wage, but she was grateful for it. Yet Phyllis knew deep in her heart that she was capable of more. She said, "I'm going to go back to school and get my high school diploma."

Her friends said, "Phyllis, you can't do that. It's too hard."

Her parents said, "Phyllis, you're no good at school. Nobody in our family graduates from school. It's too hard."

Phyllis thought, *Who says it's too hard? Who says I can't go back to school if I put my mind to it?*

Well, Phyllis not only got her high school diploma, she went to night school and got her Master's Degree. And today she's reaping the rewards of that effort. She's not on welfare anymore. No, in fact, she's a principal in the same school district where she used to collect meal tickets. Phyllis likes to say, "I went from welfare … to faring well!"

You can do something similar. Don't be blinded by "obstacle illusions." Don't listen to people who tell you it's too hard. You can go from welfare to faring well. You have what it takes. Why? Because you plus God are bigger than any obstacle.

If you really want something, go for it! Don't tell yourself it's too hard, there are too many obstacles, you just don't have what it takes. No, God would not put you in this world without giving you what it takes. If you feel like you don't have the necessary talent, ability, wisdom, or resources, simply remind yourself, *God already knows the opportunities He has scattered in my path. He has already given me what I need to succeed. It's all right there inside me.*

You are like the woman I heard about. One day she was walking into church with her husband. When she wasn't looking, the pastor gave her husband a twenty-dollar bill and asked him to hide it secretly in his wife's Bible. "Be sure she doesn't see you do it," he emphasized.

Later, during the sermon, the pastor asked the woman to stand up. "Do you trust me, ma'am?" he asked.

"Yes, of course," she replied.

"Good. Then please open your Bible, and give me the twenty-dollar bill inside."

The woman cringed. She said, "Oh, I'm sorry. I don't have a twenty-dollar bill."

"I thought you said you trust me!" the pastor said, pretending to be shocked.

"Well, I do," the woman replied.

"Then please open your Bible."

The woman opened her Bible with great reluctance, and to her complete surprise, she discovered the twenty-dollar bill within the pages. Her eyes brightened as she looked at the pastor and asked, "But how did it get there?"

"I gave it to you," the pastor said with a smile, "and now I'm simply asking you to draw out the gift I have already given, and use that twenty-dollar bill for something good."

In the same way, God will never ask you for something without first depositing it within you. God has given you everything you need. Everyday when you wake up, I want you to say to yourself, "I have everything I need. I can deal with any problem. I can overcome any obstacle." Then go out there and use the gifts that God has already placed within you.

Don't give up, look up! And, then, put up! Put up your very best effort each and every day. Life is full of obstacles, but here is what I want you to do: *Do your best, trust God for the rest.*

Do your best. Throw every ounce of enthusiasm and skill you possess into each day's work. Tackle your problems with determination and persistence. Even if the valley is dark and the outcome is uncertain, persevere. Even if you do not like the hand you have been dealt, accept it and play that hand to the best of your ability.

Then, trust God to do what you cannot do. You can only control part of the equation – the part that depends on you. You cannot control other people and their reactions to you. You cannot control factors such as the economy or employment rates. You cannot control ultimate outcomes. You can simply do your best. Then, trust God for the rest.

Of course, developing this type of trust in God's goodness is hard to do. There are several factors which make it exceedingly difficult for us to trust in God's goodness. I saw this clearly as I spent an extended time at Jesus' side.

First, there is the reality of evil. In my days with Jesus, I have seen a little girl die and a little boy thrown into violent seizures. I have seen the torment of a man who called himself Legion and I have witnessed the gathering forces of evil which were marshaled against Jesus at every turn. And, in my own life, I have seen heartbreak, conflict, and opposition to every good and worthy effort. Sadly, we live in a broken world. This is our reality. In the face of so much heartbreak and dysfunction, it's easy to doubt God's goodness.

Second, I have seen that Jesus never acts according to my timetable. In fact, by my reckoning, Jesus usually seems to show up late. Consider what these eyes have seen! I saw the distraught face of Jairus, as he begged Jesus to help his little girl. And what happened? Jesus arrived late. The girl was already dead. The funeral preparations had already begun.

I saw hunger in the eyes of the crowd and the sun sinking low on the horizon. And what did Jesus do? He blessed the loaves and fish of a little boy only after many hungry stomachs craved food.

I saw Peter accosted and embarrassed in the marketplace. "Does your master not pay the Temple Tax?" they questioned with indignation. When did Jesus pay his Temple Tax? That's right. Late.

I felt the wind in my face and the rain on my back, as our tiny boat was tossed around on the angry sea. Where was Jesus? In the back of the boat – silent and asleep. It was only after we reached the point of fearing for our lives and crying out to him with everything that was in us, that he rose to bold action. That, at least according to my timetable, was showing up … in a word … late.

Yes, Jesus does not operate on the same timetable that you and I do. He invariably seems to show up late. Yet, here is the point to hold onto. He does show up. And he does show out.

Storms are stilled. Empty stomachs are filled. Little girls are resurrected and little boys are healed.

Why does he wait so long to come to our assistance? There are many things that could be said …

He waits for us to recognize our need and call to him.

He is more interested in growing our character than our comfort.

He operates on an entirely different level than we can understand.

He does not normally override the laws of nature which he himself created and placed into effect.

He does not normally interrupt the natural cycle of cause and effect to which our actions and decisions are bound.

Yet, out of all the possible reasons, don't miss this one …

Jesus seldom does something for us that we can do for ourselves.

Why is this? It's because he loves us. He wants us to be healthy and strong, growing and mature. Indeed Jesus interacts with us the same way his Father – and all fathers – interact with their children.

Picture it this way … When I was an infant, it was natural and appropriate when my parents did everything for me. They bathed me, changed me, fed me, and even burped me! When I was a toddler, my parents naturally dressed me, tied my shoelaces for me, and picked up after me. But, as a grown man, it would be quite unnatural and inappropriate if my parents did each of these things for me. Instead, at every stage of my development, they stepped back and required more from me. In short, they seldom did for me what I could do for myself.

In the same way, our Father wants each of His children to continually be stretched and challenged. After all, He wants us to rise to our full potential – and that will never occur if we are being constantly rescued from our problems.

During my days as a reluctant "time tumbler," I repeatedly saw Jesus give people the freedom to try – and fail. I saw him allow people to struggle with hunger and heartache and loss. I saw Him allow people to do all that was within their power – and still come up short.

But I also saw that he would show up in strange and unexpected ways. When people had done their best – all that was within their power – he would show up and do that which was *not* within their power.

How does this apply to *your* situation?

My friend, maybe you're facing a situation which seems impossible. Maybe huge obstacles are in your path. But don't give up. Just do what you can do. Then, trust that He will do what only He can do. He will show up. He will show out. You will get a glimpse of His glory.

The road is rough. There are more valleys than mountaintops. But don't give up, look up! Look past those "obstacle illusions." Look to the God who is one-hundred percent on your side. Then, put up! Put up your very best effort each and every day. The secret to managing each day with inner calm and confidence is not as difficult as you may think …

Do your best, trust God for the rest.

One more word of encouragement to you …

Your situation is difficult – but not impossible.

You may feel like your problem is impossible. You've gotten the report from the doctor. You've received the foreclosure notice in the mail. You've tried to kick that habit before, but every effort has failed. Your problem is impossible.

But let me tell you this. I have looked into the eyes of Jesus. I have seen the resolve and the passion. "Nothing is impossible," he said. "Just believe."

You need to hear those very words right now. Picture him placing his hand upon your shoulder, looking you straight in the eye, and saying, "Just believe."

Perhaps you would say, "But I've just gotten the report from the doctor. The results are not good…"

Jesus will say, "Well, I'm here to bring you another report."

Perhaps you would say, "I'm out of money, out of time, and out of ideas. They're beginning the foreclosure process…"

But Jesus will say, "I'm about to begin a new process. Nothing is impossible!"

Perhaps you would say, "I've tried to kick this habit. I've been in and out of rehab…"

But Jesus will say, "This time will be different. Just believe!"

Do you remember that mountaintop where Jesus blazed with the light of another world? I told you that Peter wanted to build shelters for Jesus, Moses, and Elijah. As I rethink that moment now, I wonder if Peter was smarter than I gave him credit for.

Recall the moment with me. We arrived at that mountaintop filled with great uncertainty. Opposition to Jesus was mounting. Enemies were growing more numerous and powerful. Jesus was speaking constantly about his impending death. More than anything, we needed to know that God would take care of us – no matter what the future held.

In light of all these emotions, what were the emotions that ran deep in Peter's heart? Was Peter merely giving expression to the deepest fears we wrestled with at that moment? Or was he also expressing his ultimate trust in God?

As we met on the mountaintop, no doubt Peter's thoughts immediately jumped to a familiar experience in his past … the *"Sukkot."* Let me explain …

Every year of his life – from the time he was a tiny baby, until that mountaintop moment – Peter has celebrated *"Sukkot,"* the Feast of Tabernacles. Inscribed indelibly upon his brain and carved deep into his su+bconscious memory is the vivid experience of the week-long festival celebrated each autumn throughout the land of Israel.

Peter has crystal-clear memories of candles being lit, hundreds and hundreds of candles, illuminating every home and paraded through the streets. He remembers seeing for the first time the immense candelabra burning bright in the center of the great Temple Court. He remembers the faces of his parents in the candlelight and the excitement of his brothers and sisters. Yes, Peter remembers the joy of the season, as light swallowed the autumn darkness. And it surely reminds him of the light that cascaded across that mountaintop when Moses and Elijah met with Jesus.

To Peter and all the people of Israel, the glorious light shining out from the cold darkness of those October nights was intended to be a vivid reminder of the Pillar of Light that guided the Israelites through the wilderness on their way to the Promised Land. How Peter's imagination would soar as his parents would recount heroic stories of Moses and the wilderness wanderings. How Peter's heart would be warmed as he was reminded of how, even in the wilderness, God cared for His children. In marvelous, miraculous, unexpected ways, God was able to bring water from the desert rocks, manna from the heavens, light from the darkness, and provision for all their needs.

As a part of this annual festival, each family would build a *"sukkot,"* or temporary shelter, such as Moses and his people constructed each night during their years of wandering in the wilderness. This shelter of cloth and interwoven branches would be large enough for Peter's entire family to squeeze into. Yes, they would crowd into it like we crowd into our trailers and tents for a summer camping holiday! Then they would joyfully decorate the interior with fruit, flowers, and ornaments to celebrate the bounty of the harvest which had just been brought in – a sign of our Father's continued care and provision.

It was this type of shelter that Peter wanted to construct for Moses that afternoon upon the mountaintop. Surely Moses would want to stay in a *"sukkot,"* reasoned Peter, just as he did each night in the wilderness so long ago. Surely God would continue to care for them just as He cared for the people of Israel during their wilderness wanderings. Peter, caught up in the emotion of the moment, wanted to express with his actions what he could not express with his words: utter trust.

From start to finish, the Feast of Tabernacles is designed to express trust in God's miraculous provision and care. And the application for you and me is clear: Just as He provided for the children of Israel as they made their way through the wilderness, He can provide for us.

Like Peter, I must trust – on a deep, subconscious level. Like Peter, you must trust. You and I must trust in our Father's care and provision no matter how impossible our situation may seem.

What situation do you face? What wilderness do you wander in today? Does your problem seem impossible? God can provide what you need. It is not your job to figure out how He will do it. It is not your concern how He will work out the problem. No, it is your job simply to believe.

If you're traveling a rough road right now, if your situation seems impossible, if you're uncertain of the outcome … here is what you must do …

Just do your best, and trust God for the rest.

Yes, there are more valleys than mountaintops. But don't give up, look up! God has a plan – a plan of unwavering goodness and love. He will work out the problems. He will fit the pieces together. All things will work together for good in your life. And He will do for you what you cannot do for yourself. Sure, there will be some obstacles along the way. But you plus God are bigger than any obstacle. That is why …

I am The Ultimate Optimist!

Key Discovery
Become The Ultimate Optimist.

Part Five

Entry 16

Arrest

I lie in bed, my eyes open, staring into the darkness. Beside me, Kathy is asleep. I hear her soft, rhythmic breathing.

I wish I could sleep, but my thoughts are racing. My mind won't turn off. I hear Jesus' voice echo in my head: "Just trust me."

I do trust him. I do believe that a plan exists. But the problem is, I'm clueless as to even the most basic outline of this plan. I'm in the dark, out of the loop. Yet I'm the one who has to make decisions that will affect the future of my family and my church. I'm the one who has to answer to bankers, provide direction to staff, and set a course for the church.

And I am flying blind.

To quiet my mind, I intentionally draw in a deep, cleansing breath, hold it momentarily, then attempt to exhale the stress from my body. I consciously slow my breathing and relax my muscles. I close my eyes, shutting out the world around me. Then I begin to silently repeat all the promises I can recall from Scripture, willing peace into my troubled mind.

"The Lord is my shepherd,
I shall not want…"

"Surely goodness and mercy
shall follow me all the days of my life…"

"All things work together for good
for those who love God…"

"Nothing can
separate us from the love of God." [26]

Instantly I'm aware of the smell of fresh earth and dry leaves. The air is filled with the drone of crickets. And the deep, rhythmic breathing beside me is no longer Kathy's.

I sit bolt upright, trying to catch my bearings.

The breathing belongs to Peter, who is sound asleep beside me. John and James are a few feet away, both sleeping with arms crossed over their chests and backs resting against the twisted trunk of an ancient olive tree.

We're in a large grove of olive trees, a secluded farm enclosed by an ancient stone wall. In the distance, across the rocky plunge of the Kidron Valley, I see the lights of Jerusalem glittering silently beneath the full moon.

A stone's throw away, I see Jesus. I want to run to him, greet him, throw a friendly arm over his shoulder and feel the warmth of his smile.

But something is wrong.

I've never seen Jesus like this. His agitation is clearly visible. All of his power seems to be gone; he is crushed, beaten, broken.

"My Father!" he cries out, frantic, cornered.

I hear despair, dread.

He falls to his knees, like his legs have been kicked out from under him. "Oh, my Father …" His voice chokes back a sob.

Then Jesus – the one who can still a storm with a word, the one before whom angels bow and demons tremble – falls face forward onto the dry earth. He lies on the ground like a worm, stretched out, clutching fistfuls of dirt, crushed beneath an immeasurable weight.

He speaks few words, but they are spoken in agony. "Father, nothing is impossible for You. Nothing!" His voice rises. "If You are willing, Father, take this cup from me!" His voice climbs to a crescendo. "Father, I don't want to drink this cup You are giving me!"

And now his halting words fall to barely a whisper. "But ... not my will ... but Yours ... be done."

Jesus drops his face into the dirt, powerless. After a wordless moment, he turns his head to the side. Suddenly, his eyes open – open wide! – as if staring into the light of another world. His breathing slows. His face grows calm. Slowly, he sits up. He stares off into the distance. Then, slowly, ever so slowly, he stands.

The twisted olive branches form a perfect arch over him, like the curving vault of a medieval cathedral. Just then the full moon breaks from behind a passing cloud, throwing its pale light into the ancient grove. Jesus stands silently between the rows of shadowed trees, like a crucifix standing on an ancient altar between two flickering candles. Slowly he holds out his hands, as if waiting to be led away.

Jesus turns his face toward me. His face is dark with sweat and soil. The whites of his eyes gleam in the darkness. Our eyes lock. Neither speaks a word. He just looks at me with a dread too deep for words.

At that instant, a large military detachment streams through the eastern gates of Jerusalem and pours down into the steep, rocky ravine of the Kidron Valley. I see a long line of torches and lanterns glittering in the night, flowing slowly in our direction. I hear the rattle of their equipment and the cadence of their measured march as they draw closer.

Jesus moves quickly about the garden, rousing the others. His tone is different now. There is strength and control. There is confidence. "The hour has come," he announces. "All of you, up! It's time!" He pauses momentarily and looks from face to face. "I'm about to be betrayed." He points out over the Kidron Valley. "Look, here comes my betrayer."

His words drive every trace of sleep from our eyes. Even this heavy-lidded group can now see the approaching lights and hear the growing noise. We grasp that something fearful is about to happen.

While we are still speaking in hurried whispers, the first soldiers arrive at the entrance of the walled grove. We look from one to another with growing dread as the detachment swiftly surrounds the entrance. There'll be no easy escape.

My heart is pounding, my mind racing. An out-of-control, fight-or-flight panic is spreading among us. We look to Jesus. What should we do? We're surrounded. There must be two-hundred soldiers from the Roman legion – and certainly at least as many Temple police! With them is a noisy mob that has followed along to see the excitement.

Even more shocking is the one who leads them. It is a familiar face. A brother. A best friend. One who rode beside us in our boat that night on the stormy sea, who napped with us in the soft grass of the hillside on that perfect spring day, who distributed the baskets of fish and bread to the hungry thousands. It is one of our own …

Judas.

Judas acts overjoyed to see Jesus. "Greetings, Rabbi!" he exclaims loudly so that all the soldiers and police may hear. Without hesitation, he steps forward and throws his arms around Jesus, slapping him on the back heartily.

Without giving Jesus a chance to respond, he leans forward to greet Jesus with a kiss. It is customary in this culture to greet a friend in such a way – I've seen it many times. It's a sign of friendship, warmth, and honor. But there is something strange, something awkward and over-the-top, about the kiss of Judas. He kisses Jesus not just once on each side of the face. Instead he showers Jesus with kisses, honoring him excessively, as if to shout to the soldiers, "Yes, this is the man you want!" His extreme show of affection only serves to highlight his black betrayal.

Immediately the Roman commander orders his men forward to arrest Jesus. Steel scrapes against steel as swords are drawn from their scabbards. Torches lunge through the blackness as soldiers spring forward. They are upon us in a heartbeat.

A soldier's rough hand grabs at my arm. I swing my elbow wildly, frantically, connecting with his throat before I am brutally thrown to the ground. I feel a knee in the small of my back, as my arms are pulled sharply behind me. I scream in a blinding flash of pain, feeling as if they are ripping my arms from their sockets. The taste of blood and dirt fills my mouth as my head is driven into the ground.

Peter goes down beside me. He frantically hammers his captor with his fists, and leaps up. In a flash, Peter has his own sword out, swinging wildly. He lands a blow, drawing first blood. The man reels backward. I see blood streaming down his face.

But Peter, an untrained fighter, has merely severed the man's ear. He has not taken him out.

The panic is contagious. Those still standing fight only to be free, only to save themselves. It's every man for himself. They struggle to escape the grasp of their captors and then run headlong into the darkness, directionless, one this way, one another. One of our group, Mark, slips frantically out of his robe as a soldier clutches at it. He runs off into the darkness, naked.

Only Jesus remains calm. Only Jesus remains in control. While the storm rages around him, he remains supremely confident at its center. Holding out his hands to his captors, he announces, "I am the one you are looking for. I am the man."

They swiftly converge around him. His hands are forced behind his back and tied tightly.

Now only Jesus and I remain in the hands of the captors. The others have managed to escape, fleeing into the darkness.

While still pressed into the ground, my hands are tied securely behind my back. Then I'm roughly hoisted to my feet, the pain streaking through my shoulders as they yank me from the ground.

I'm pushed next to Jesus, my balance awkward, my feet scuffling and kicking up dust. Jesus turns to me. He locks his eyes upon mine.

I see the same look ... the same look in his eyes that I saw on that night upon the lonely hillside, overlooking the sea. It was exactly one year ago. Earlier in the day Jesus had fed the thousands. That night we talked, one on one. "Do you love me?" he asked. "Then follow wherever I lead."

That night, the full Passover moon darted in and out from behind the clouds, sending glittering shafts of light over the black sea. I look up.

Now, on this night, the moon hides behind the clouds. [27]

I'm in a stone courtyard. I've been up all night, standing, waiting. I'm exhausted. My feet ache. The coppery taste of blood fills my mouth. My arms are still secured tightly behind my back. My shoulders are on fire. It's been twelve hours since my arrest. *Please, someone, just let me lie down.*

But I am an afterthought. An accident. A footnote. Jesus is the real focus of attention. He's been grilled all night, first by one magistrate, then another. He barely speaks. When witnesses bring testimony against him, he looks them in the eye. Yet he speaks not a word in his own defense.

Through the night we've been dragged through a procession of palaces and meeting chambers, through a parade of illegal hearings and sham trials. Names that will one day darken the pages of history, because of this night, have become real to me: Herod, Caiaphas, Pilate.

Now soldiers grab Jesus from behind, yanking him backward by his hair. He loses his balance and stumbles awkwardly. Taking hold of his arms, they drag him toward the west corner of the courtyard, where a thick, low stone pillar stands. They quickly strip Jesus of his robe and under garments, leaving him naked and exposed. Jesus is strong and well-muscled, but I am surprised by how thin he is. He looks vulnerable. He looks defenseless. His captors, surrounding him, look larger than life, encased in their bulky Roman armor.

I try not to look. I don't want to witness what is about to happen. But I cannot shut my eyes.

The soldiers bend Jesus forward across the coarse stone pillar, with his back stretched and exposed. In order to hold his body in position, they tie his hands and feet to iron rings which are fastened into the stone pavement.

Immediately a soldier steps forward with a whip, and then a second. They are in no hurry. They uncoil their whips slowly. They make sure Jesus sees what is coming. They enjoy the power they hold over their victim.

Both soldiers hold a short-handled whip, each with several leather lashes imbedded with bits of sharpened lead and bone. They slowly, mockingly, move the lashes back and forth before Jesus' face. Jesus turns his eyes to me, but I say nothing.

Now the captors move behind him, out of his line of vision. Then it begins. Out of nowhere the first lash whistles, streaks through the air, and cracks into his shoulders. The slashing fingers rip into Jesus. The jagged bits of bone and lead bury themselves in his body. As it is ripped backward, I hear an audible tearing of skin. I see the bright red claw marks left by the stinging, slashing cat-o-nine-tails.

Then the second soldier swings his lash. Again, the whistle, the crack, and the ripping away.

The soldiers come at him from both sides. They lay the strokes with full force. The centurion is shouting, "*Adde virgas*! Put some life into it!" and "*Firme!* Harder!"

The effect is horrible. His skin and flesh are gashed to the very bone in every direction. Each stroke pulls away strips of tattered skin. Where the lead and bone strike, deep punctures pour dark, crimson blood. I see exposed ribs, tattered tissue and tendon.

Jesus cannot help it. He writhes about on the stone pillar. He tries to pull his knees up to his chest. He tries not to flinch. With each blow, I hear a low guttural cry, a primeval cry, a cry not quite human.

Now darkness seems to close in upon Jesus. His eyes turn up in his head and he slumps down, unconscious.

Yet still the lashing continues. Still the cries fill the air.

Only then do I realize – the cries come from me.

All the while, more men are gathering. Some race through the garrison, shouting and alerting as many off-duty soldiers as they can. This should be quite a show, they claim, a bloody diversion to break up the tedious hours of their routine.

Soon the barracks are empty and three to four hundred soldiers are crowded tightly into the courtyard. All are ready for the show – yes, a bloody show like something they'd see in the Roman arena!

Jesus is unfastened and his naked body slides from the pillar. His face hits the stone pavement hard. Soldiers roll him onto his back and a pail of water is thrown in his face, making him choke, cough, and sputter. His eyes blink open.

Immediately, he is hoisted to his feet. For a moment, Jesus has trouble standing. He sways, unbalanced, then finds his footing.

"He claimed to be the King of the Jews!" charges the centurion in command of the garrison. "Let us pay homage to the king!"

A soldier brings out an old worn cloak, once crimson, now faded and dirty. The cloak is thrown over the shoulders of their victim. Jesus flinches as the rough, soiled cloth is pressed into the raw wounds on his back.

"But, wait! Surely such a glorious king deserves a crown!"

Another soldier uses his dagger to cut branches from a thorny bush that grows in the courtyard. From these twigs, he creates a crown, a crown that bristles with thorns. The crowd parts, making way for him to approach their victim. Jesus watches the soldier draw closer as if watching from a great distance.

The soldier bows deeply – a great mocking bow. Then he places the horrible, jagged crown upon Jesus' head. As he presses it into place, trickles of blood begin to run down Jesus' face. Blood – mixed with tears.

Yet this royal robe and crown need a final touch. Every king must have his royal scepter! A wooden staff is thrust into Jesus' right hand. Now the king is dressed for his part!

I have seen artists' depictions of this moment. But none have come close to what I am seeing now. There is no beauty and majesty in this moment. There is only stark, brutal reality. This is blood, tears, and cruelty. This is torture.

Jesus is pushed into the tightly packed crowd of soldiers. They shove him from person to person. They make a great show of bowing before him. "Hail, King of the Jews!" they say with a flourish.

As they heave him through the crowd, someone grabs the staff from his hand and strikes him brutally across the face. At once, the tone of the crowd turns from mere mockery to blood-lust. The shoving becomes rougher. He is thrown this way and that. He staggers, unbalanced. Blows are showered upon him with the scepter, each driving the thorns deeper into his flesh.

Then, in the very center of the crowded courtyard, they stop. A soldier ties a blindfold over his eyes. The beating immediately resumes with a new intensity. They slap him right and left, turning him this way and that, calling out, "You are supposed to be a prophet! Tell us who slapped you!" Again and again fists rain down upon him. "Prophesy!" they demand. "Who hit you?"

When Jesus refuses to answer, their anger grows. They spit in his face. It is the greatest humiliation yet. Great gobs of saliva cling to his beard, mingling with his own mucus and tears.

The King of Kings stands before them naked, but for his cloak and crown. His nose is bleeding. His face bruised. His eyes swollen nearly shut. His back shredded.

The King of Kings … can barely stand.

"Enough!" shouts the centurion. "Dress him and drag him out into the square!"

In a dramatic billowing sweep, the scarlet cloak is removed and Jesus' own robe is thrown over him. With a shove from the soldiers, he lurches forward.

Now, I feel rough hands grab my arms, pushing me forward as well. I'm several paces behind Jesus, but catch up quickly. After all, he can barely walk. He stumbles forward as if his robe is woven of lead and, try as he might, he cannot stand straight beneath its unbearable weight.

We walk between our guards. The centurion leads the way. The sea of soldiers parts for the centurion as he moves through the courtyard. He's the commander of a hundred soldiers, and he radiates power as he moves through them.

I am directly behind Jesus, not beside him as I want to be. We walk beneath a low stone archway. Above us, soldiers watch from stone towers that soar above us on either side of the gateway. As we pass through the darkness of the low, shadowed gateway into the bright sunlight of the public square, a thunderous cry explodes from the crowd which has gathered to see the death of Jesus.

Roman law requires prosecutions and sentencing to take place in public. In order to pronounce a legal judgment, the Roman governor, Pontius Pilate, will sentence Jesus in this open square rather than within the safe confines of the ancient stone fortress.

At the sight of Jesus, the crowd explodes into a frenzy. "Crucify him! Crucify him!"

They surge forward, close enough for me to smell the stench of sweat and sour breath.

Jesus is half pushed, half carried, up the steps of the *tribunale,* the wooden platform upon which Pilate sits to deliver his judgment. I remain at the foot of the platform. I am not important here. I am an afterthought.

As Jesus reaches the top of the steps, Pilate rises from the Judgment Seat and stretches out his hand toward Jesus.

"Look at this man!"

Jesus tries to stand straight and square his shoulders, but fails.

"Here is your king!"

The crowd erupts with ferocious shouts. "Take him away! Take him away! Crucify him!"

Pilate acknowledges the crowd's demands.

"Shall I crucify your king?" shrieks Pilate.

"We have no king but Caesar!"

The huge crowd is quickly spinning out of control. They are a mindless mob. They are careening toward a riot. Their fists pound the air as they begin a rhythmic chant: "Crucify! Crucify! CRUCIFY!"

Soldiers form a line before the platform to hold them back.

"CRUCIFY! CRUCIFY! CRUCIFY!"

The noise is deafening. Earsplitting. Guttural.

"CRUCIFY! CRUCIFY! CRUCIFY!"

Pilate sinks down into his Judgment Seat. Gripping the armrest of his chair uneasily, he delivers his verdict.

Jesus will be crucified.[28] The execution is to be carried out immediately.

I have not moved and I hold my breath as Jesus' fate is sealed. Beside me, a soldier speaks, shoving me forward.

"And what about this one?"

Pilate turns to look at me. Without a thought, he answers.

"Crucify him."

Entry 17
Cranium

God, no!

My heart pounds. I sway, fighting to stay upright. I feel like a man who is hit by a rogue wave on the ocean's edge. I'm fighting just to stay on my feet, catch my breath, keep my head above water.

Oh, God, no. This can't be happening. Please, God, do something! Get me out of here! I don't belong here.

I try shaking my head violently. I know I'm asleep right now, in my own bed. I must be. I know my wife lies next to me, warm and soft. I know this can't be happening.

But it is.

This is happening.

I lunge backward, trying to break away. Clearly I have no plan; I am simply reacting. I lash out in a panic. As the soldiers seize me, I try to break away from their grip with the intensity of a drowning man fighting for air.

The guard on my left is the first to take hold of my arm. I ram him with my shoulder. With all my might, I kick at him. My hands are still tied tightly behind my back, so I lower my head and use it as a battering ram. All I know is: I need to run. I have to escape. No matter what it takes.

Soldiers immediately converge around me, swiftly drawing their swords. One strikes me across the face with the blunt side of his sword, and I reel sideways, taken off my feet. As I attempt to rise, another plunges his knee into my stomach, knocking the wind out of me. I crumble to the stone pavement of the courtyard. My futile attempt at resistance is rewarded over and over again with a flurry of kicks from the soldiers that surround me. I try to curl into a fetal position. *My back! My ribs!* Light explodes in my skull, as a final kick pounds my head against the stone pavement. My body goes limp.

I'm hauled to my feet. My hands are untied. I can't move my arms. For more than twelve hours they have been tied tightly behind me. My arms are stiff and unyielding.

My guards, working together as a team, thrust a thick beam of wood over my shoulders. It's the crossbeam, the *patibulum*, to which I will be nailed.

Because I cannot lift my arms, the guards forcibly wrench them upward to hold the beam in place. Fire shoots through my joints. There is no mercy. What consideration I might have earned from the soldiers disappeared the moment I tried to fight them off. They quickly retie my arms, this time wrapped over and around the crossbeam. I bend beneath its weight.

With renewed vigor, I repeat my internal pleading for this to end.

Oh, God, don't let me be stuck here! I should be asleep in my bed now...

I think of my wife. *Kathy, will I see you again?* Panicking, I wonder: *If I die here, will I be dead there, too?*

The words that keep pounding in my head turn into a prayer ...

Oh, God, don't let me be stuck here ...

Oh, God, don't let me be stuck here ...

Oh, God...

I'm pulled from my thoughts when the shadow of a soldier darkens the ground in front of me. He steps up to me and hangs a crude wooden sign around my neck.

"Latro," it reads. "Thief."

So that's the charge they came up with? I'm a thief? That's what they're telling the world?

The sign knocks against my chest as I lurch forward, shoved by the soldiers.

We are paraded through the public square, then northward, through the narrow streets of Jerusalem. A large detachment of soldiers clears the way. We are walking into a sea of people. The angry mob parts as we wade in, then they stream along behind us. At least one other criminal is pulled from the fortress and marched into the streets with us as well. A detachment of four soldiers is assigned to each of us, the condemned. In addition, a large force is ordered to accompany the execution detail, to ensure that the crowds don't get out of hand.

As I stumble through the ancient stone streets, a hellish cacophony surrounds me. The rabble shouts their insults. Shopkeepers heave their rotten fruit and refuse. Women follow us, shrieking, pounding their breasts with closed fists, wailing the mid-eastern death cry, for we are as good as dead. The sound of wailing women … When was the last time I heard this sound? Was it in the home of Jairus? Yes. That day held a resurrection. What will this day hold?

I lower my head and concentrate on the ground directly in front of me. I see the sandaled feet of the soldier immediately in front of me, just within my range of vision. I focus on that. I try to block out the noise that surrounds me and the future that awaits me. I will concentrate on taking the next step. I can do that much. I can take another step and then another. I hear the slapping of the soldier's sandals on the stone pavement and I keep moving forward, each step an effort.

I'm already weak from the beating. I've been denied food and water. I've been on my feet all through the long hours of the night, deprived of sleep. Now I'm bent beneath the crossbeam. My back and shoulders are on fire. But I manage to walk forward beneath the weight.

Not so for Jesus. He falls repeatedly. In fact, I'm surprised he remains upright at all. I struggle; but for Jesus each step is a Herculean effort. Now he falls and can go no further. The centurion in charge of this detachment pulls a random on-looker from the crowd and orders him to carry the crossbeam for Jesus.

At last, we reach the edge of the city. I see the great, grey wall that surrounds Jerusalem. It towers above us, timeless and impregnable. We pass through the Garden Gate, but still the road winds on. Now the wall is on my right. On my left are small homes and simple fields, outlined with low fences of piled stone running in every direction.

I look up, wondering how much farther I'll be forced to march. The answer is directly before me. Just ahead is a small rounded hillock, a rocky mound already pierced with several bloodstained poles, each ready to receive its next victim. Here, the crossbeams and the bodies of the condemned will be lifted into place. I will be nailed to my *patibulum* here.

And I will die here.

This hill, resting beside a main thoroughfare just outside the city gates, will provide for good public viewing. Because of its skull-like shape – and because of its deadly purpose – this hill is known locally as "Cranium."[29] The Romans who drive us forward call it by its Latin name …

"Calvary."

As we reach the crest of the hill, the entire detachment grinds to a halt. The soldiers behind me untie my hands. As my arms drop, the heavy crossbeam thuds to the earth. The centurion hands each of us a small clay bottle filled with liquid. "Drink!" he orders. It's a drugged wine: a cheap, sour wine mixed with myrrh, a narcotic.

Jesus refuses it. He will go through this day clear-headed.

Not me. I place the jar to my lips and drain it.

As the accompanying soldiers hold the crowd back in a semi-circle around the execution site, the four soldiers assigned to me begin their task. They work quickly. The sooner their work is complete, the sooner they can return to the safety of the fortress.

Four soldiers surround me and strip the clothes from my body, leaving me naked and shivering. My humiliation is now complete. I try to cover myself. But still the crowd – both men and women – calls out their taunts.

Without warning, the soldiers trip me. They have clearly done this before. Their efficiency, even in this, astounds me. Two thrust me backward, while another trips me with his leg. I fall hard upon the well-trampled ground.

Wordlessly, a soldier grabs each arm. They drag me headfirst across the stony ground. I try to escape, twisting my body and kicking at them, scuffing up clouds of dust. Someone lifts my head by the hair, then drops it down. My head hits the wooden crossbeam with a thud. Then they yank my arms right and left, palms upward, as far as they will stretch. A soldier kneels upon each arm, pinning it in place, while another sits on my legs. I can't move. A final adjustment is made to the positioning of the crossbeam beneath my shoulders.

I feel a cold point pressed against my wrist. An iron spike is moved about, probing, indenting the soft underside of my wrist. The soldier is seeking the perfect place for the spike. He finds it: the thin opening between my wrist bones.

I look up. I see the unshaven faces and the hulking forms of the soldiers who pin me in place. I see the cloudless blue sky, distant behind them. I turn my head to the side and shut my eyes tight.

Just then, I hear the crack of the mallet upon the iron spike, metal upon metal. I hear the dreadful thud – once, twice, a third time. I feel my wrist bones separating and then I hear the metal bite into the wood of the crossbeam beneath me. A cold, dull pain courses up my right arm and into my neck.

I hear screaming. Someone is shrieking, someone far away. It's the sound of a dying animal – wounded, howling, crazed.

My left arm is nailed in place in the same way.

It is then that I realize that the screams ... the screams are mine.

The dying animal is me.

My eyes fly open. My head is reeling. Is it the narcotics, now pouring through my veins? Or is it the horror of being impaled?

My God, I'm pleading, *why must I endure this torture?*

Then, I'm hoisted upward, lifted entirely off the ground. For a moment, I'm airborne, dangling a few feet off the ground, swinging by my arms alone, supported only by my impaled wrists. By a show of sheer strength, the soldiers muscle me into place, my body raised against one of the permanent fixed poles that line the crest of the hill. The *patibulum* slides into the pre-cut notch in the fixed pole and settles into place with a thud. A soldier raises a ladder, speedily climbs to my head level, and lashes the *patibulum* securely in place.

The cross is now formed.

Soldiers seize my legs, bend my knees, and place my right foot flat against the thick upright pole. Next they cross my left foot over my right. A third spike is driven through my ankles. I scream until my voice is raw and ragged.

My body convulses. My stomach heaves. Bile fills my mouth. I begin to tremble, my limbs twitching as if I've been out in the cold. Yet my body shines with sweat, baking in the mid-eastern sun.

I look over at Jesus. He is now raised into place. A mocking cheer erupts from the crowd.

"Father, forgive them." His voice is gentle as he speaks. "They don't understand what they are doing."

In response, those within the sound of his voice explode with a violent ferocity, hurling their derision at him. "Come down from that cross if you are the Son of God! Save yourself!" they taunt.

Even the officers of the Temple join in. "He saved others," they sneer. "Let him save himself!"

From all directions, ridicule is flung at Jesus. "Let him come down from the cross now and we will believe in him, too! He trusts in God! If God wants him, let God rescue him!'"

Even I begin to shout at Jesus. Is it the drugs? Is it the influence of the jeering crowds? I am in a panic and I need to get his attention. I need his help. I cannot understand why he has abandoned me. "Jesus!" I shout.

He does not even turn in my direction. His head hangs limply, his eyes fixed upon the ground.

"Jesus!"

I am desperate – desperate to escape this nightmare, desperate to return to my own century, desperate to return to my warm bed.

I scream louder, my own voice unrecognizable to me. "How can you say you love me? How can you turn your back on me? How?"

Now the other criminal, on the far side of Jesus, joins in. He, too, shrieks at Jesus. His words become even more caustic and cutting. Perhaps it is this, this verbal attack, which shakes me out of my panic. I know that Jesus has done nothing to deserve this, and I can't remain silent.

I turn on the other criminal. "Don't you fear God?" I roar. "You are under a death sentence – and you are getting what you deserve! But this man has done nothing wrong!"

Now my heart goes out to Jesus. I remember him with the children. I remember him holding the hand of Jairus' little girl. I remember the sunny spring day on the side of the hill, overlooking the sea.

I speak, uttering words that tumble from my heart.

"Jesus, remember me when you come into your kingdom."

Only now does he turn toward me. Finally, he gives me his attention. He locks his eyes upon mine. A moment passes between us. He speaks.

"Today you will be with me in paradise."

Time is without meaning to me.

I slide in and out of consciousness. Pain throbs and courses and flows with each beat of my heart. I am floating in a stream of pain. I am carried in a current. I am drifting. I shut my eyes.

When my eyes open, the shadow of my cross has moved.

My labored breathing worsens by the minute. Putting all my weight on my impaled ankles, I push myself upward, straightening my legs.

There. I can breathe better. I can fill my lungs with air.

But now my feet and ankles are searing. The cold, dull throb has become a white-hot fire.

My legs are trembling violently. I cannot hold this position. I settle downward again, letting my wrists bear the weight.

I feel the muscles in my chest cramping.

I close my eyes again.

The current carries me away.

When I open my eyes, I am in darkness. *Is it night? How long have I been unconscious?* My breathing is raspy. I can't fill my lungs. I need air. I am drowning. I am drowning in thick, deep darkness.

Blood courses down my wrists, little rivulets pumped with each pulse of my heart. Flies swarm around my mouth and eyes. I can't brush them aside. My hands are pinned.

I am thirsty. Oh, God, I'm thirsty!

My tongue is swollen and stuck to the roof of my mouth. My lips are cracked. Each breath burns deep within my lungs, a fire inside me.

I look over to Jesus. I try to speak. A croak comes from my throat, little else.

Is he still alive? His body hangs limply, his head drooping forward.

Just then, he raises his head. In a show of unexpected strength, he pushes himself upward upon the cross, straightening his legs. I watch him through the deep, dense darkness. With his arms outstretched, nailed in place left and right, he looks like he is holding out his arms to embrace the world.

As I watch, he draws in a great breath and roars a single sentence …

"It … is … FINISHED!"[30]

The single-sentence proclamation is delivered in a tone of a triumph. Though everything about this scene speaks of darkness and defeat, a smile rises upon his lips, a brightness like the first glimpse of the golden sunrise over the darkened horizon.

Those watching turn their heads.

Jesus no longer appears defeated. Bloodied and battered though he is, he exudes supreme confidence. His pronouncement rings with self-assurance and buoyancy. It is the same Jesus I have always known. He has spoken from the cross with the same tone he used that day in the boat, as he called out to the storm to be still. I almost sense relief in Jesus, as though he has now, at last, accomplished a long sought after achievement.

Though I have not enough strength left to string a sentence together, Jesus has rallied. He possesses a wellspring of physical and emotional strength which I lack. I am utterly without reserves. Because of this, I feel completely unprepared for what I see next.

Jesus pushes himself high upon the cross. His back is straight, his head high, his chest out. His muscles stretch and flex, his arms and chest defined. Without a single shred of weakness, he lifts his face skyward. Then he calls out in a loud voice, "Father!"

All eyes turn to him.

"Into Your hands I commit my spirit."

He immediately draws in a great breath of air, filling his lungs to capacity. I see his chest expand outward, his ribs defined even in the darkness. Then, with clear intention, he exhales – one final, great, breath of air. As he exhales, his head lowers and his body goes limp.

At that moment, the very earth beneath us begins to convulse. The ground rolls like waves upon the sea. The ancient city shudders. My cross sways violently, then settles to the right. All at once, the remaining onlookers shriek and reach out their arms, wildly seeking their balance. Some curse, some pray, as they tumble over like a child's wooden blocks.

The centurion, tasked with this execution, reaches out to steady himself, placing a hand against my cross. Looking up at the still face of Jesus, he speaks to no one in particular.

Yet he speaks the words we are all thinking.
"Surely this man was the Son of God."

I am borne away, carried on an ink-dark current.

Jesus is gone. I am alone. He has left me.

Each breath burns, a swift-moving brush fire. I am lost, feverish, floating, carried by the current, as dreams and reality intermingle without form.

The darkness is thick. A jagged spear of lightning pierces the sky, flashing over the ancient city. I am crying, I think – no tears find their way to the surface.

My breath comes in quick, shallow pants. My body has lost all control of its functions. I soil the ground beneath me.

Agony.

Torment.

Torture.

"I need to breathe…"

I push myself up, feeling the cool air fill my lungs.

Just then, a soldier arrives with updated orders. I watch him make his way across the hilltop, which remains as black as night. He locates the centurion. The order is given to immediately perform the *crurifragium*, the breaking of the legs, a brutal hastening of death. I overhear the final words of the orders being given: "… that their legs might be broken and their bodies removed immediately."

What? *What?* My clouded mind is having trouble making sense of these words. *Legs broken? Bodies removed?* I watch a soldier proceed at once to the cross of the convict on the far left, directly opposite me. The soldier lifts a great hammer of wood and polished stone, the same hammer used to drive the iron nails through me. In a mighty arc, the hammer is smashed into the shin bone of the convict.

The condemned man screams horribly, a guttural, animal, preternatural scream.

Then the other leg is broken.

His body hangs heavy. The crucified man can no longer push himself upward on the cross to open his airway and expand his lungs. Death will come soon now – a choking, wheezing, terror-filled death by asphyxia.

Now, the soldier turns in my direction. I can't turn away. I watch him cross the dark, stony hilltop. He takes several steps toward me, but stops momentarily at the cross in the center. Looking up at the gray corpse that hangs heavily, he can clearly see the *crurifragium* is unnecessary. The victim is already dead. Rather than the exertion of swinging the heavy hammer, he simply takes his spear in hand and, with a quick thrust, plunges it into Jesus' heart. As the spear tip is pulled back out, a mixture of blood and pericardial fluid pours out, a sure sign to the soldier's battle-trained eye that the bodily fluids have settled and a beating heart has stopped.[31]

Jesus is dead.

At last the soldier stands before *me*.

Oh, God.

From my cross, I look into my killer's eyes. Then my eyes dart quickly to the hammer. I watch the hammer. I fear the hammer. I fear the terrible explosion of pain as my legs are shattered.

A gargle erupts from the man on the far cross. He is struggling.

The soldier toys with the hammer, feeling its smooth handle and dreadful weight. He winds up, pulling the heavy hammer airborne. Then, with a heaving grunt of exertion, he swings it in a terrible, mighty arc.

I catch my breath … my eyes wide … my lips forming a scream.

In a blur, the hammer sweeps through the thick, oily, charcoal-black air.

As it crashes into my leg …

I crash …

Into another world …

A world unlike anything I have ever seen.

Entry 18
Light

    I am standing in a wildflower-dappled meadow, bathed in golden sunlight. The water from a mountain brook tumbles over ancient stones, sparkling and glinting with diamonds of light. A soft breeze moves over the meadow, bending the grass in lazy waves.

    One second ago I was drowning in thick darkness. Now my eyes must adjust to the brightness. There is an intensity, a brilliance, a vividness to all my senses. The sky looks more blue, the meadow more green, the sunlight on the water more shimmering than I have ever seen.

    More than that, my mind must adjust. I fall to my knees and push my face into the jade-green grass, breathing in its earthy scent. I run my fingers through it, feeling its textured softness. *Is this real?*

    I no longer hear the soldiers, the screams, the death struggle of the dying criminal – all that has echoed into oblivion. The din that filled the darkness is gone. I no longer feel any pain – the torment is gone. I have broken free of its current.

    Is this what death is? Am I dead?

    Just then, I see a large dog – a black lab, it looks like – bounding over the crest of the hill. The dog runs directly toward me, romping and bouncing through the tall grass with the joy of a pup, its tail wagging with uncontained excitement.

As the dog grows closer, I see a familiar diamond of soft white fur on the jet-black chest ...

It's Jet, my own dog when I was a boy! Jet, who remained my inseparable companion through all my growing years, who died of old age when I was away at college. I learned of her death during my freshmen year, in a letter from my mom. Tears welled in my eyes as I read the news in my dorm room. My last memory of Jet was the morning I left home for college. As I loaded my things in the car, she watched from the window, her muzzle white with age, her eyes filmy and rheumy.

Now Jet is bounding toward me with the joy and energy of a puppy. Her sturdy leg muscles ripple as she runs. Her eyes are unclouded and her fur is black and sleek. She leaps the rocky brook in a single bound, and then she is upon me.

As I kneel, she laps at my face and presses herself against me, her tale wagging outrageously. "Good girl!" I exclaim. "Good girl! Beautiful girl!" I pat her back heartily and take her face in my hands.

Just then, another figure clears the crest of the hill. This time there is no doubt who is striding toward me. I'd recognize that familiar gait anywhere.

It's Jesus.

This is not the Jesus of the cross, ashen and broken. This is the Jesus who walked the countryside with me, the Jesus who lifted the children onto his shoulders and played with them on that perfect spring afternoon, the Jesus who taught the crowds beside the sea. And this Jesus is ... more.

As he reaches me, his smile lights up – and the old fireworks light up inside of me. He runs his hand along Jet's sleek, shining, jet-black fur, and says, "I had to let her run ahead – she was just so excited to see you!"

Then Jesus wraps me in a huge hug, a hug all muscle and masculinity, all fists and joy, a hug like one soldier would give another, after the long battle is over – after death was near and there's life to be lived.

I notice the scars on the wrists of Jesus, battle scars, deep scarlet, but healing nicely. Then I look down at my own wrists. I have them, too – thick ribbons of red. I hadn't noticed until now. There is no sensation of pain or rawness, not even the itchy discomfort of healing. They're now nothing but an emblem from the past, like the colored ribbons that adorn the chest of a soldier to mark past campaigns.

"Follow me," says Jesus. "I want to show you what lies on the other side of that hill."

We begin walking up the gently sloping meadow. Jet romps along beside us, stopping often to sniff at an interesting scent, then racing ahead, turning often to be sure we're following.

As we reach the crest of the hill, my eyes are overwhelmed with a sweeping panorama. A gleaming, soaring city of glass and gold and sunlight rises before me. How I hadn't seen it before, from the other side of the hill, I'm not sure. Surely it must have filled the horizon, from one end to the other!

The city seems strangely silent. I hear none of the sounds usually associated with a bustling metropolis. Even the road leading into the city is entirely empty. *Is the city abandoned?*

I look over to Jesus for an explanation. He simply shrugs and says, "Let's go take a look…"

And so we hike down the far side of the hill, a strange little band – Jesus, Jet, and Jeff. And, as we walk, we talk. Jesus and I talk about the events we shared over the past week and there is much to be said. We talk about Peter, and how frightened he must have felt. We talk about Thomas, and chuckle over his stubbornness. We talk about John, and how touched Jesus was by John's unswerving friendship. But, mostly, we talk about the ordeal we shared. We will never forget this past week; no, not for as long as we live. We compare stories – what was going through our mind when; what part seemed the worst; yes, what we had lived through, died from, and come out the other side better for. While we talk, Jet prances along proudly.

Soon we are at the edge of the city.

The silence seems unnatural.

We're standing before a soaring gate, a gate which appears to be carved from a single immense pearl. The towering entrance yawns open before us. Though we just passed through a meadow that is golden and bright with sunlight, an even greater light shines out from the open gate. The light highlights each detail of the intricately carved pearl. Whatever is on the other side of that gate … whatever it is, it is resplendent … glorious. It must be!

Is this heaven? If so, where is everyone?

Jesus and I walk through the gate, into the shade of its covered passageway, the echo of our footsteps splashing across the pearly walls and low stone ceiling. Jet trots along beside us, her feet padding on the ancient stone. Still we see no sign of anyone.

Jesus is the first to emerge on the other side. He is awash with light. Without breaking his stride, he turns to motion me forward, his face emblazoned.

I step through the stone gateway into a wide, broad plaza…

And, at that very moment – in a moment I will never forget, no, not for the rest of eternity – I am struck by a deafening roar! From every corner of the plaza, from every open window, people yell, "Surprise!" The sound rolls over me like the thundering crash of a white cap rolling up upon a rocky shore.

I look over to Jesus. He throws his head back with laughter and claps his hands together with exuberance. Joy just seems to spill out of him!

A great throng of people – more than I can count – cheers my arrival. They call out their congratulations and clap their hands. I hear them say, "You made it!" They gather all around me. "You're here!" I feel them slap me on the back.

Just then, I see my parents, in the very front of the crowd. My mom is laughing. My dad, who I have never seen cry, is wiping tears away. My parents are young and strong, more youthful than I myself appeared the last time I looked in a mirror. My mother's face is unlined. My father's once thinning hair is again dark and full. They bound forward and throw their arms around me.

"Were you surprised?" asks my mother.

"That's an understatement!"

"We thought it would be more fun this way!" she exclaims, laughing with excitement.

Beside them, I see my grandparents. They're strong and beautiful, more alive than I've ever seen them. I spot a friend I've not seen since high school. We swore we would never lose touch, but of course we did! I point to acknowledge that I see him, and wave. Just then Peter steps from the crowd. I see James and John directly behind him. How happy I am to see them! Yes, they have made it, too! They smile with a joy that could light the entire city!

Just then I feel hands patting my back boisterously. I turn to take a quick glance over my shoulder and I see my children – my proud sons and beautiful daughters! They call me "Pops" and "Old Man" and tease, "It looks like they let anyone in here!" They are all here with me – they surround me, beaming, laughing, sharing the biggest moment of my life!

And who else is with them? A wonderful group of people, all of whom love me, not one of whom I have ever met. They are my future grandchildren and great grandchildren. Introductions are made – introductions that shatter my own perceptions of my life. There is an avalanche of love and respect and honor that is tumbling over me. Never before had I the slightest conception of the richness and fullness of my life. My view of my own life, up to this point, contained only a fraction of reality.

One young woman whom I have never met leans against me, her arms wrapped around my waist. She looks vaguely familiar, kind of what a young woman would look like with my dark eyes and Kathy's petite frame. "Were you surprised, Gramps?" she purrs.

"I guess you have already met Liz," offers Jesus. "She's a grandpa's girl. You two will spend hours together. You will be very close. You two have this way of communicating without even saying a word."

What will the future hold for this girl? Or is it the past?

I am introduced to a young man who looks very much like me. "I'd like you to meet David," says Jesus. "You never knew David. He never spent time on earth outside the womb of his mother."

"But I don't ... I don't remember ..."

"You never even knew about David. But, here on this side of eternity, you two will be especially close. You see, he not only looks like you, he has your sense of humor. You two will be inseparable – two peas in a pod! Some people might think of a miscarriage as a 'loss.' Here we see it as just another lucky 'find.' You will discover quite a few surprises await you here!"

There is much hugging, much laughter, much love – so much love. Indeed I have never felt such love. If I were to take all the love I have ever felt in my entire lifetime, each moment sweet and wonderful, and press them together into a single experience, it would not equal one second of the love I now experience here. I am bathed in love: pure, perfect, and unconditional.

There is just one person missing ...

Just then, another surprise: Kathy steps out from behind my parents.

She bursts from the crowd and steps toward me, opening her arms. Our eyes meet and the love I feel for her cascades, spills over and over, and flows between us. I rush toward her, burying her in my arms. She snuggles against me and for just a moment there is just the two of us. She looks up at me with beautiful blue eyes which reflect the sky of heaven.

"Well, we wanted to give you a moment that you would remember forever," she whispers. A sudden smile lights her face. "We all know how you love a good story to tell!"

We're holding hands, surrounded by family and friends, surrounded by love.

Jesus puts a hand on my shoulder to get my attention. "Jeff, this way! Follow me! You'll be able to get a better view from up here!"

Jesus leads me toward a series of steep steps, carved of pearl. I am still holding Kathy's hand. Taking the steps two at a time, effortlessly, we wind our way up the ancient stairway to an elaborate ceremonial platform perfectly centered above the carved gate.

Stepping out onto the platform, a cheer rises again from the throng. Jesus raises his hand and waves, acknowledging the praise. Then he takes hold of my hand – and raises it into the air. The plaza again echoes with cheers, as still another wave rolls forth.

With this one small gesture, my heart does a somersault within me. How like Jesus! He has done all the work – from Bethlehem to Calvary – yet he freely and completely shares every ounce of the glory with me. What words could possibly speak more clearly about the kind of friend he is to me? What simple gesture could better reveal the personality of the Lord I have learned to love?

From here on this platform, perched above the crowd, I can see more of the City of Light. The first thing that strikes me is the breathtaking beauty of this city. I see the fingerprints of the Creator everywhere! I rub my hand over the intricately carved railing of the balcony, feeling the smooth evanescent pearl. I see architecture, artwork, and parklands that completely fill my senses. Every inch contains the beauty and creativity of a thousand masterpieces on earth. I look over at Kathy, and we just shake our heads in wonder. Truly this is paradise, the paradise that Jesus, from the cross, promised to share with me!

As the home of our Father and the capital of His Kingdom, the wealth and the splendor of this city are beyond that of any empire that has ever risen. The outer wall is constructed of rusty-red jasper that shines as bright as flame, the inner city of burnished gold. Precious gems of every kind are inlaid in the walls, creating intricate patterns and sweeping colors exploding outward in every direction. I see brilliant blue sapphire that sparkles like the Caribbean Sea, rich purple amethyst that drapes buildings with the appearance of royal robes, topaz as sheer and transparent as white wine, and so much more. Colors – more colors than I knew existed – are filling my senses. Everything, everywhere, in every way, captures light, emanates light, radiates light. The entire city glitters like glass, sparkles like crystal. Somehow even the simplest buildings refract light like a prism, shining with a spectrum of color beyond the limited spectrum available to our eyes on earth.

Like my vision, all my senses are not just pure and perfect, they are heightened. I see colors I have never imagined; I hear music more beautiful and emotional and evocative than any I have ever heard; I feel my body pulsating with life and strength and health. Indeed I quickly begin to realize that my mind is functioning at a level unlike anything I have ever experienced. Ideas that I had perceived only dimly now strike me with crystal clarity. Concepts that were clouded are now entirely transparent. Moreover, my thought patterns contain none of the weaknesses which once darkened and polluted each thought and impression. I am utterly without fear, jealousy, or pettiness. My mind is void of hurt or pain or regret. Removed of this sludge, my thoughts fly lightning-fast with astonishing creativity and intensity.

I am also struck by the vastness of the City of Light. Buildings soar to heights that I would consider impossible. Well-ordered streets stretch out in every direction, pulling my eyes to new wonders wherever I turn. Beyond the sweeping plaza into which I was welcomed, I see a wide, peaceful river which flows through the center of the city. Along its banks are strange and beautiful trees, trees whose branches hang heavy with fruit unlike any I have ever seen. They call this unknown species "The Tree of Life," I am told, and all are welcome to eat of its fruit.[32]

I could tell you more, so much more. But Jesus asked that I not ruin *your* surprise! Moreover, to try to adequately describe this remarkable afternoon is impossible. It would be nothing more than a feeble attempt to describe the indescribable. I could no more describe color to a man born blind than describe heaven to a man born earth-bound. Yet I can tell you this much. The greatest pleasures and joys found on old earth are merely a tease compared to the pleasures and delights of heaven – much like the appetizer before the feast or the sneak preview before the featured film begins. Truly, what we experience on earth is but an inkling, a whisper, a hint of the reality that awaits us.

Maybe I can make sense of it to you this way .... Have you ever been hungry, so hungry that your stomach growls and your mouth waters at the thought of food? Imagine being in your own living room, feeling that kind of stomach-growling hunger, while you smell your mom's best cooking being readied in the kitchen. You can see the rolls, fresh from the oven, steaming and waiting for butter, already placed upon the table. You can smell the spaghetti sauce. You can see the table all set with dishes. Then, your mom asks you to come into the kitchen. She hands you a spoon and asks you to taste the sauce and tell her what you think. How good that little taste will be! How intense! And yet it is not the meal, it is simply a taste. In the same way, all the pleasures we experience during our entire lifetime on earth are merely a taste of the wonderful feast God has prepared for us in the future!

I remember the words spoken to me from the cross. "Today you will be with me in paradise."[33] Was that just this afternoon? After all I have seen and experienced, I can't believe it's the same day!

Or is it?

There's a timeless quality to this afternoon. The City of Light! So much to explore! So much to absorb!

I turn to Jesus. "When can we see our home?" I ask, squeezing Kathy's hand in excitement. "I know that you have prepared a home for us."[34]

In truth, I feel completely at home already. In fact, I feel as if this is what I have been homesick for all my life, though I never understood it.

Jesus pauses momentarily, the first shadow that has crossed his face since we have arrived.

"Jeff, you can't stay," replies Jesus.

"But I want to stay. I don't want to go back. No, not ever. This is … home."

Jesus places one hand on my shoulder and the other on Kathy's shoulder. "I have a beautiful place prepared just for you two. It's all ready. I chose everything myself, just for you, and I loved doing it! It's just perfect for you … but it's not time yet."

At this moment, everything within me wants to remain. I don't want to go back – back to the land of grayness and shadows, of trouble and turmoil.

"But …"

"Jeff, you and Kathy still have things you must complete."

So it's settled.

I see things clearly now. Those who live in those earth-bound, time-bound, shadow-bound lands on the other side of eternity call this the "afterlife." From this day on, I will never again call this the "afterlife." No, not at all. This is "Life" itself.

Instead …

I will call my days on earth …

The "beforelife."

"There is one thing that confuses me," I say to Jesus. "Time."

"Time?"

"Yes."

This business of leaping through centuries in a flash has puzzled me. Of course, I want to understand how it is that I can be in my office or in my kitchen one second – and a fraction of a second later, after only a moment of disequilibrium, I can find myself in an entirely different time and culture. Was this really happening? If so, is there an explanation I can wrap my mind around? I want to give it a shot …

I push the idea forward with Jesus. "Okay, it's Friday afternoon, just after three o'clock, right? At least it was when I was on the cross. Then, in the next fraction of a second, I was here, walking in that meadow. But …" I pause, trying to straighten this in my head. "But, a fraction of a second before that, it was night, I was in my bed, Kathy was sleeping beside me, and twenty centuries had slipped away."

My mind is swimming. "Now, as far as I can figure it, I am somewhere on some other side of eternity. The people I love are here, though as best I can make out, not one of them has even been born yet. In fact, whole generations of my grandchildren and great grandchildren, not even born yet, are here with me with their entire lifetimes on earth already completed. It makes my head spin!"

"Jeff, you have difficulty with this because you have spent your entire life bound by time. This is all you have ever known. In your experience, you are locked in time like a person locked in a railroad car which is continually rolling down the tracks. As far as you know, you cannot free yourself from this railroad car. And, try as you might, you cannot stop that car from barreling along."

"Okay, but …"

"But here's where it gets interesting: I hold the key to that railroad car in my hand. I can free you. I can free you to move from car to car, exploring and enjoying each one at your own pace, as you wish."

"Okay," I mutter, a glimmering sense of awareness just beginning to dawn. "But … but I feel like I'm tumbling from century to century. It's not like I'm walking from one car to the next in any orderly fashion. No, I flash from the front of the train to the back of the train instantaneously."

"That's because I'm plucking you up and putting you down somewhere else entirely. Think of it this way … Picture the entire scope of human history, measured out century after century. Imagine if you could fit all of human history on a single yardstick, with each littlest fraction of an inch equaling another century, each inch another epoch. Here, in this tiny half-inch, the Romans rule the world. There, in this other fraction of an inch a little to the right, Queen Victoria sits on her throne. Here, at this far end, are events that have not yet occurred in your frame of reference. You – and every human being since the dawn of time – live your entire life in the tiniest fraction of an inch imaginable, in a space that cannot even be seen by the human eye."

Jesus pauses to see if I am keeping up.

"But, Jeff, I am not locked into living in this yardstick. It's more like I stand above it, able to watch each inch simultaneously, looking here and there, across the whole yardstick at once. I can watch Queen Victoria at the same exact moment as I watch you. This is no problem for me – just as it would be no problem for you to use a yardstick."

"But I'm still confused. You're telling me that you can see everything all at once ..."

"Yes, everything."

"So, no matter what time or place, culture or century, you're there, equally present, equally aware, totally on top of things? It's as easy for you to do this as it would be for me to look down at a yardstick and take in the whole yardstick at once in my line of vision?"

"Yes."

"Wow. Well, that explains how you know so much. You know, the 'all-seeing,' 'all-knowing' thing. I get it. But that doesn't explain how you can be personally involved in all things. There's a difference between *seeing* what's happening and being *involved* in what's happening."

"Okay, Jeff, let me explain it another way. And please understand that every analogy falls apart at some point – especially when I'm trying to explain something so big to someone with such a small mind."

He smiles as he says this – but I know he is right! Even here, with my mind working at incredible levels of clarity and capacity, there are things that my limited mind cannot fully grasp. There are things about time, space, and reality that are beginning to dawn on me – but that even here, even now, Einstein could not fully fathom.

"Okay, Jeff, let's make this simple. People in your culture often think of time as being like a river. It is always flowing. It is unstoppable. You think of yourself as being carried along by it. But, the simple truth is, right now at this very moment, you and I are standing on the banks of that river. We're not in it. We're not being carried along by it."

"Okay... But ..."

"But, Jeff, we have the ability to stick our hand into the water any time we want. Picture this: As we stroll along the riverbank, we can stick a toe in the water at any point we desire. Or we can stick a hand far beneath the surface to really swirl things up. We even have the power to dramatically alter the direction of the flow. In fact, the truth is, we can wade completely into the river wherever and whenever we feel like it."

"Do you do this often?"

"You can't begin to imagine! Take for example that sleepy little village called Bethlehem … that was me – slipping quietly in! Or take that amazing day when the Red Sea parted at just the right moment … that was me – making a splash! Or even that idyllic first morning in Eden, at the dawn of time, as light fled from darkness and stars exploded into space and Adam first stood and stretched …. That was me – playing like a child! Even what your culture calls 'the Big Bang' was nothing more than what I call 'doing a cannon-ball!'"

"Incredible. Absolutely incredible! So you're telling me that you can watch over everything and you can be a part of everything."

"Exactly."

My mind is moving quickly now.

"Then why would we ever be afraid? I mean, if you love us and you want nothing but the best for us … and you are aware of what we're going through at every moment and you can be there with us to help us … why would we ever be afraid?"

"Now you're beginning to see."

"What I see is that life is so much better than we ever imagined! Everything, in every way, is better than anything we have ever dreamed! You're there helping us all the time, arranging things, putting things together – whether we can see it or not." I pause for a moment to take in the wonder of it all. "If only I could help people in the 'beforelife' see what I'm seeing right now. If only I could help them feel what I'm feeling …"

"But, wait, Jeff. There's still more – so much more. You're only beginning to scratch the surface. Yes, life is so much better than you have ever imagined. And you have not yet seen the best of it! Let me show you. It's time for you to slip into that river again. Hold your breath … you're going in … and it's going to absolutely take your breath away!"

With that, like two boys playing at the side of the pool, Jesus pretends to give me a playful push. As his hands touch me, I tumble …

through time …

just in time.

Entry 19
𝕯𝖆𝖗𝖐

I cannot see.

I am trapped in pitch blackness. *Underground? A cave?* I smell dirt, stone, and staleness. The floor beneath me is hard.

I reach out my hand into the blackness and feel cold, damp stone. *Am I in an underground prison?*

The air is cold, but there is no breeze.

No, there is not the slightest movement of air. Nor is there the slightest trace of sound. I can hear my own heart beating, my breath drawing in and out of my lungs, my digestive juices gurgling in my stomach. But nothing else. It's like I am standing in a sound vacuum.

I feel about, running my hand down the length of the wall. I seem to be in a stone chamber which is perhaps six feet square. The low ceiling looms less than a foot above my head.

Feeling with my hands, I follow the wall, groping in the blackness until I find an opening cut in the wall. I feel my way through a low doorway into a second small chamber. I trace the contours of a low stone shelf running along the base of the wall, the size of a park bench.

Suddenly my hand falls upon something cold and clammy.

Oh, my God! It's a body! Oh, God!

I feel toes, ice cold and unmoving, and jerk my hand away. I've stumbled upon a corpse. A shudder wracks my body with fear and revulsion. I lunge backward in the darkness, stumbling back through the doorway into the first chamber.

But now I notice something, something that was not there before. There's a small sliver of light pushing through a crack in the wall. I make out the outline of a thick stone doorway. Is the sun rising on the other side, sending its angled light upon the entrance? Or are my eyes gradually adjusting to the darkness, growing accustomed to the loss of heaven's light?

I'm buried alive, sealed in stone, entombed in the darkness with a decaying corpse. *Oh, God!*

I push at the stone door, trying to escape from the chamber. I kick at it and heave my shoulder against it. I try to pry it open, squeezing my fingers into the tiny crack. I'm close to panic. But it's no use. I cannot come close to budging it. I look around, hoping to see another way of escape.

In the faintest of light, I see the corpse. Stretched out upon the stone shelf, it is wrapped in linens. I move toward it with a morbid curiosity.

I carefully pull back the linens from the face.

It is Jesus.

Oh, Jesus, what have they done to you?

His eyes are swollen nearly shut. His nose is broken. Someone has hurriedly washed the blood from his face, but the deep puncture wounds are still everywhere visible from his thorny crown.

Oh, Jesus.

The hands that healed are now still and cold. The eyes that looked with compassion are now sunken and rimmed with shadows. The face that lit up each time he saw me is now as cold as marble and as pale as alabaster. The one who promised to show me paradise has now vacated his place in it.

I want to hug him. I want to take his hand. I want to comfort him. But I'm repulsed. He is dirty. He is decaying. He is death.

And so I stand silently above him, afraid to touch him.

And then it happens – suddenly, without warning – though I should have expected as much.

The earth itself heaves forward. I clutch at the wall to remain standing, as the ground beneath me shudders and kicks. I feel an intense pressure in my head; my ears are instantly blocked. And then …

There is an explosion of light, thick like liquid, blinding and fearful. Energy cascades outward from the corpse at the speed of lightning. I am bathed in brightness. I am swimming in light.

Suddenly the fists which were still and lifeless … clench. The eyes which were vacant and sunken … blink open. A great breath of air is drawn into the awakening lungs and, with a loud gasp that shatters the stillness of the tomb, the corpse … breathes. With the limberness of a child awaking from an afternoon nap, the corpse … sits up.

Jesus slides his legs from the stone shelf and puts his feet firmly on the floor. He is breathing normally. His face is resolute and alert. He begins to unwrap and carefully refold the linen burial cloths which bind him. He folds the shroud neatly and places it to the side, where his head was resting.

Already a rosy hue is returning to his face. Jesus exudes life. He overflows with vitality. Strength and health and energy spill out of him. *Jesus is the most alive man I have ever seen!* As he stands and stretches, he reaches over and squeezes my arm affectionately. I smile wildly, full of wonder and excitement and awe.

Just then, a deep grating rumble fills the tomb. Slowly at first – very, very slowly – I see sunlight spilling into the darkness. First it is just a small silver sliver. I see tiny dust motes floating in the still air, as if in slow motion. Then the opening grows brighter, as the great stone slab which blocks the entrance to the tomb is rolled back along its track. Sunlight washes into the tomb.

Suddenly, in one huge dramatic burst, the great stone is flung backward, out of its track entirely. It flies some distance from the tomb, rolls once, then thumps down heavily, kicking up a cloud of dust.

As the tomb opens wide, I look outward. From my vantage point inside the darkness of the tomb, the small, rectangular opening of the doorway looks like a framed picture of another world. I see the sunrise, pink with flecks of gold. I see the sun pushing over the distant horizon, a blazing red ball, resting in a cottony blanket of gold.

And I see heavily-armed Roman soldiers, more than a dozen strong, face down on the ground, their arms shielding their faces, their swords lying at their feet. I see them leaping to their feet and fleeing frantically away from the tomb, running headlong from the burial garden.[35]

Now a young man steps into the doorway of the tomb, stooping low to look inside. He shines with the light of another world, enrobed in dazzling white. Even his face shines as bright as a bolt of lightening, brighter than the rising sun. He is taller than me and fearfully muscled. He looks at me with deep, expressive, blue eyes as he bends low to enter the tomb. Another Being of Light, equally radiant, follows behind him. Both stand in the doorway, speaking not a word.

Unlike the Roman soldiers, I am unafraid in their presence. I feel no urge to flee. They are angelic beings. I understand this. I saw many like them when I visited the City of Light. I know they are servants of the King and they will not harm me. They, too, are here to witness this day.

Anxious to be out of the cold darkness of the tomb, I step through the opening of the tomb into the pale morning light. The

187

soldiers are gone. The morning is still, but for the chatter of birds. Already the golden Judean sun is beginning to warm the day.

Now Jesus emerges from the tomb. He is all health and life and joy and unexplainable things. It is as though a river of life flows through him, coursing and cascading out over the world in an unstoppable current. The two Beings of Light stand on either side of him, an honor guard for heaven's king.[36]

Jesus strides directly over to me. With a nobility that I have never before completely recognized, he speaks without hesitation. His words brim with confidence. In a voice that shines with victory and triumph, he proclaims loudly, "I am the resurrection and the life!" A wide smile spreads over his face. "Anyone who believes in me will live even if he dies!"[37]

I understand these words as never before. I am an eye-witness to these words. I will speak these words with new passion and force at every funeral, at every hospital room, at the side of every freshly-dug grave I ever visit.

Then Jesus reaches his hand forth, like a king reaching for his scepter. But instead he touches me. "Because I live you will live also."[38] The words are spoken quietly. But the words carry a power which is unmistakable. This victory, won this day at so great a cost, will spill over onto me.

And onto you.

Now flecks of gold burn like fire in the eastern sky.

The angels have departed, but Jesus asks me to wait at the tomb. Just as he did almost a year earlier, when he asked me to wait behind and dismiss the crowd while he went on ahead into the hills, he leaves me behind with specific instructions. I am to ensure that the message of what happened here this day reaches the right people.

I wander back, stepping into the shadowed chambers of the tomb for a closer look. The entrance, cut into the face of a natural limestone embankment, is large enough to enter without crouching. It is a rich man's tomb, spacious and unsparing. As I enter, I see the first room, the room in which I was fumbling about in the darkness earlier. Now sunlight spills in through the entranceway, bathing the room in gold. This room appears to be a small outer vestibule rather than the actual burial chamber. It's a room designed for family members to gather quietly to mourn the loss of a loved one. Then, to the right, is the actual burial chamber. It's a small stone cell with benches cut into the base of the walls for mourners. The shelf where the body of Jesus lay still holds his neatly folded grave cloths. I see rolls of linen, stained and saturated. I see the burial shroud, burned and bloodied.

For a moment, I sit down on the shelf where the corpse of Jesus rested, trying to gather my thoughts. I have lived lifetimes in the past twenty-four hours! I have traveled to unimaginable worlds on the far side of eternity! And I have lived and died – and lived again! More than that, I have been an eye-witness to the single greatest event in the history of the world. And now, I'm struggling to fully grasp its implications.

What I have witnessed will have already sent shockwaves through the cosmos. Like a large rock being dropped into a still pond, it will send out waves of life in all directions, through all millennia. Unable to adequately comprehend the scope of this cosmic event, I reduce it to something I *can* understand. It is this: Death is not final. Heaven is real. Jesus wins. That is what this all means. And, with a sudden realization that floods my heart with emotion, I understand one simple fact …

I will spend eternity with the people I love.

Lost in these thoughts, I am completely startled as I hear the shuffling of sandaled feet at the entrance to the tomb. A woman bursts through the opening, excited and confused. She is immediately followed by two of her friends. They are astonished to find the stone rolled away from the entrance. As their eyes adjust to the darkness of the interior, they see me seated to their right.

It's completely reasonable for women to be startled when confronted by the presence of a large man, a stranger, surprising them in an unexpected place. But they seem absolutely terrified to see me in here! One women lets out a small, sharp shriek, another puts her hand to her chest as if her heart is about to stop. Alarmed, all three quickly back away toward the exit.

"Wait! Don't be afraid!" I quickly speak up. "You're looking for Jesus, right?" They stop. I have their attention. "He's not here. He is risen!" Their eyes grow wide with fear and confusion. "Look!" I say, pointing quickly, "there's the spot where they laid his body." Their eyes dart to the stone slab and the folded grave cloths.

I continue on quickly, trying to convey the necessary information before they lose their nerve entirely and race out of the tomb. "Go and tell the disciples that he is alive and already on the move. He's going ahead of them into Galilee. They'll see him there, exactly as he told them before he died!"[39]

Before I can say one more word, the women turn on their heels and flee from the tomb as quickly as their trembling legs can carry them. It is then that I realize what a strange sight I must be: Such a strange man in such a strange place! They had come carrying burial spices, expecting to say their final tearful goodbyes to a man they loved, expecting to gently wash and embalm his body. They had worried only about convincing the guards to roll away the stone from the entrance for them. Instead they find an open grave, a missing body, and a stranger lurking in the shadows.

It is then that something more dawns on me, something filled with mystery and wonder. I notice strange shadows upon the walls – shadows that seem to be cast from a light that emanates from me. I hold my hands out in front of me. I turn them over and over, amazed. My skin, my clothing, my very presence seems to shine with an unearthly light. Even as the shroud seems to have absorbed the light and the energy that exploded forth at the moment of the resurrection, I have as well. I am shining with a dazzling light, white and bright. I feel amazingly young and strong. I feel healthy and brimming with life. It is as if I have somehow absorbed a wave of the life-force that exploded in this chamber this morning.[40]

I think of the paradise in which I had walked earlier. Remembering the indescribable light, I realize that I look like a citizen of that resplendent city more than I look like a creature of earth.

And then it dawns on me … the answer to a mystery which has stood unanswered for twenty-one centuries. The Gospels clearly record that there were two angels present on this day – Beings of Light, bright and dazzling. But, mysteriously, the Gospel of Mark adds a puzzling statement not recorded by any of the others. Mark writes of a young man being present that day … inside the tomb of Jesus … a young man who shone with the light of another world! It was this unnamed young man who delivered the first news of the resurrection to the women who came with their embalming spices just after sunrise on the first Easter morning.[41]

And so, once again …
I, a simple Twenty-First Century man …
a husband and a dad, no different than a thousand others …

have somehow …
unintentionally …
inexplicably …
mysteriously …

entered the ancient pages of Holy Scripture …
as a central player in events …
that occurred twenty-one centuries before I was born.

Entry 20
Fall Guy

So, I guess you could call me "the fall guy."

I stumble across centuries, trip through millennia, fall headlong.

I am the fall guy.

I experience a shift in equilibrium. I lurch into another century. It is outside of my control.

But I must now show you the identity of …

The True Fall Guy.

The one who deserves this title – I mean, truly deserves it – is Jesus.

I did not choose to leave my comfortable home. I did not choose to leave my wife and children, my friends and job, and all that I've ever known, in order to slip into a different time and culture. It just happened. Inexplicably. Uncontrollably. Like a sudden sneeze.

And I certainly did not choose crucifixion. No, this was never a choice I would make. I somehow stumbled into these events, got stuck, and I was unable to get out. That's the long and the short of it. I was stuck.

But Jesus *did* have a choice. He chose to leave the City of Light and fall headlong into the darkness of this world. He intentionally chose a rustic little village called Bethlehem to make

194

his entry. He purposefully chose a rugged lifestyle. And he knew from the start that it would end in a bloody, brutal death.

For this, he is the ultimate Fall Guy.

Yet there is more, so much more. He intentionally did this to "take the fall" for us.

The Bible says, "Jesus himself carried our sins in his body when he died on the cross ... by his wounds we are healed."[42] Wrap your mind around this profound fact: He willingly absorbed into himself the sin and guilt of the entire world. Then he bore the punishment for it on the cross. In other words, when Jesus died on the cross, he was "taking the fall" for us.

You say, "But, Jeff, why did he have to go through all that? Couldn't there have been an easier way to take care of our problems? Couldn't there have been an easier way for God to make a statement? Why did he have to *die?*"

I have thought about this a great deal. Obviously, the crucifixion is seared into my mind. Obviously, I cannot escape it. For me, this is more than a cold, academic, doctrinal truth. Like a survivor of the horrors of war, suffering post-traumatic stress, I try to make sense of it all. Here is what I have come up with. Follow me on this ...

God is fair, so He must punish wrongdoing.

God is always fair. God is always just. And justice and fairness demand a consequence for every action. For example, if someone gets caught cheating on a test, there must be a consequence. It's only fair. If the teacher said, "Oh, well, that's okay," what would the other students in the classroom say? "That's not fair!" they would protest. "I had to study hard for that test!" It would clearly go against our sense of right and wrong if the teacher just overlooked the offense.

As human beings, we have a well-defined sense of justice. If someone backs into your car, they should have to pay for the repairs. That's fair. If someone breaks into your house, they should go to jail. That's fair. If someone does something wrong to you, they should be punished. That's fair. Yes, we have a very strong sense of this – and so does God.

The problem is, you and I have done some things wrong. Therefore, by all rights, God must punish *us*. You see, not one of us is perfect. No, not one of us.[43] And, even if we fool other people, we don't fool God. God sees exactly what we're like …

It's like the cute story of the husband and wife who are getting ready for bed one night. She is standing in front of a full length mirror taking a hard look at herself. "You know, honey," she says, "I look in the mirror and I see an old woman. My face is wrinkled, my chest is down to my waist, and my bottom is a mile wide. I've got fat legs and my arms are flabby." She turns to her husband and says, "Say something good about me." He thinks for a moment and then says, "Well, there's nothing wrong with your eyesight!"

And there is nothing wrong with *God's* eyesight. God sees us just as we are – all the blemishes, imperfections, and scars. All the sins and failures and mistakes of an entire lifetime. God is fair, so He must punish wrongdoing. But there is another truth which is equally powerful …

God is merciful, so He wants to help us.

God sees us just as we are. He is just and He must punish sin. Fairness demands it. But He's also compassionate. He deeply loves us. So He found Himself in a dilemma. *His justice demands that our sin be punished; His love desires to help us.* So, to stay true to Himself, God decided to do something amazing. He decided to send His own son to us as "the fall guy." Jesus became a human being and came to this earth for one reason: so he could pay the price of sin himself. He took upon himself the punishment for every sin of every person who has ever lived. He took the hit. He "took the fall."

What does the Bible tell us?

The Bible says: "Jesus died once and for all – the innocent paying for the guilty – to bring us back to God."[44]

The Bible says: "When we were utterly and completely helpless, Jesus came at just the right time to help us …. Yes, this is how God demonstrated His great love for us: He sent Jesus to die for us, even though we were sinful!"[45]

The Bible says: "For God so loved the world that He gave His one and only son, that whoever believes in him shall not perish, but have eternal life."[46]

And finally: "The wages of sin (that is, the payment we deserve for our sin) is death; but the gift of God is eternal life through Christ Jesus our Lord."[47]

Could the Bible be any clearer?

Jesus is the Fall Guy.

There is a story about a king who had only two laws. The first was that all people should honor their father and mother; the second was that they were not to steal from one another. One day it was discovered that someone in his kingdom was stealing. The king immediately called his people together. He said, "Let the thief come forward and receive ten lashes for this crime." No one moved. So he upped the ante to twenty lashes, then thirty, and finally forty. He stopped there, knowing it would take a strong man to survive forty lashes.

Since no one owned up to the crime, the king sent soldiers to scour every corner of the kingdom in search of the criminal. One week later, they returned. In shock, the king watched as soldiers dragged his own mother before him. His mother was the thief. His heart broke for her.

Now the king was faced with an impossible dilemma, one that tore at every fiber of his heart. Would he follow the law and punish his own mother? Such an action would surely kill her. Or would he show mercy and let his mother go free? If he let her go free, no one would ever respect his law again.

One week later, the king again summoned the people. Before a great assembly, he watched as his own mother was tied to the whipping post. As the whip master raised his arm to administer the forty lashes, the king walked to his mother and tore the shirt off his own back. He then draped his own body over her body, and he took the forty lashes himself. The king was, at one and the same time, both just and merciful.

This is what Jesus did for us. The price for our sins had to be paid. Justice demanded it. So he paid for us. He took the hit. He suffered in our place. Every single time the lash tore into Jesus, he was bearing it for us, as that king did for his mother. In short, he intentionally "took the fall" for us.

He is the Fall Guy.

God's *justice* demands that our sin be punished; God's *mercy* desires to rescue us. On the cross, in a single event, Jesus satisfied the demands of both *justice* and *mercy*. But there is one more thing you need to know about God's personality.

God loves you, so He will do whatever it takes.

The reason Jesus came to earth is simply this … He loves you. It was love that pulled him from heaven, drawing him to our world. It was love that held him to the cross, not nails.

In fact, the Bible says that God loves you more than a mother loves her own child.[48] Think of the fierce love a mother has for her child …

Years ago a young mother was caught in a blizzard with her infant son. A search party went out and crossed the land looking for her. Finally, they found her. She was frozen to death, clutching a little bundle. Inside that tiny bundle of cloth was her infant son, alive and healthy. She had removed her own clothing, wrapped it about her baby to keep him warm, and given her life for his.

She loved him, so she did whatever it took.

That child, history would later reveal, would grow up to become the Prime Minister of Great Britain. His name was David Lloyd George.

She loved her child more than her own life. And that is how God feels about *you*. The question is: How will you respond to that love? Will you love Him and trust Him? Will you open your life to Him?

Maybe life has knocked you down. He wants to build you back up. Maybe someone you loved and planned to build a life with walked out on you. God will never walk out on you. Maybe someone turned their back on you and said they no longer love you. God will never stop loving you.

My friend, it is impossible to exaggerate the love God has for you. It is a love that will pay any price.

I heard about a little boy who built himself a toy boat. He carved it with loving care, fashioned a sail for it, and painted it with beautiful bright colors. Then he took it to the lake on a breezy day, put it on the edge of the water, and gave it a push. The wind caught the sail and the little boat darted along the surface of the lake. The boy clapped his hands together in delight.

Unfortunately, a gust of wind suddenly caught that little boat and swept it out of his reach. He jumped into the shallow water and grabbed for it, but it was no use. The boat was too far away. He helplessly watched it sail until it was out of sight – gone. That was a sad day in his young life, for he loved making that boat and didn't want to lose it.

One day, while walking through town, he saw a boat in the window of a toy store. It was his boat! He ran into the store and said to the shopkeeper, "That's my boat in the window! I made it. You can even see my initials carved into it. Thank you for finding it."

But the shopkeeper said, "You can't take that! That boat is mine now. Somebody came in here and sold it to me. You can buy it back if you want, but it will cost you twenty-nine dollars."

Wow! That was an enormous amount of money for that little boy. The boy went home and collected every coin he could find. He emptied out his piggy bank. He did extra chores for mom and dad, until he finally had enough money. Then he went back to the store, put the money down on the counter, and said, "I'll buy that boat."

As he walked out of the store, with the boat tucked under his arm, he was heard saying, "You are mine now. You are my boat twice over! First, because I made you. Second, because I bought you."

Do you know what? God says the same to you. However far you may have drifted from God, you are God's child and He loves you. In fact, you are God's child twice over! First, because He made you. Father God created you in His image and carved His initials into you. Second, because He bought you. On the cross, He paid a steep price to bring you back.

You say, "But I've really made a mess of things. I've made bad choices. And I really haven't paid much attention to God. Do you think God loves someone like me?"

My friend, there is no one in the world who loves you the way God loves you. You may think your parents love you, or your husband or wife. But I tell you, you can multiply their love ten-thousand times ten-thousand and it will not equal the love that God is feeling for you at this very moment.

You argue, "But why would God love someone like *me*?"

You might as well ask why stars sparkle and shine in the night sky. Stars can't help shining, and God can't help loving. It's just who He is. It's just what He does. God is love. And God loves *you*.

"Even me?" you insist. "But I come with a lot of baggage, a lot of regrets, a lot of problems."

Yes, even you.

Still your doubts and insecurities call out to you. "But, I've committed some big sins. Can God love me – in spite of my sins?"

My friend, God's love is bigger than any sin you can commit. It's like tossing a handful of sand into the ocean. The ocean is big enough to absorb the sand, and God's love is big enough to absorb your sin.

Maybe you're a lot like that little boat. You've drifted away from God. You've been away from God for a long time. But God has never stopped loving you. My friend, today is the perfect day for you to come home. Father God will welcome you like a favorite child.

In the quietness of your heart, just say, "Father, I want to come home. I am sorry that I have drifted away from You. I am sorry for my sins and mistakes. But I trust in what Jesus did for me on the cross, when he took the fall for me. I don't understand it all. But I surrender as much as I understand about myself today, to as much as I understand about You today."

God Himself will speak the "Amen" to that kind of prayer.

In the great cathedral in Copenhagen, there is a beautiful statue of Jesus. And there's a story behind that statue. About two-hundred years ago, an artist was commissioned to create a statue depicting Jesus. He wanted it to be a masterpiece. He was determined to portray Jesus as the king of kings and the master of men. He made him heroic in size, his head thrown back like a conquering emperor, his hands raised in a gesture of command.

When the artist completed the statue in clay, he was very pleased with it. So, he locked the doors of the studio and went out for the night to celebrate. There was just one thing he forgot to do: he forgot to shut the windows. That night a fog swept in off the ocean and worked a strange transformation upon that artist's clay.

The next morning, the artist returned and he found that Jesus' head had fallen forward and His hands had lowered into a gesture of pleading. The artist was horrified! But, as he studied the statue, a transformation began in his own heart and mind. He said to himself, *Maybe this is more like the real Jesus. Maybe he was not so much the Conquering King, as the Lord of Love.* So, he made only one small change. At the base of the statue he inscribed the words of Jesus: "Come Unto Me."[49]

To this day, that is exactly the way that statue stands in the cathedral of Copenhagen. And that is exactly the way you will see copies of that statue in churches and gardens and cemeteries the world over. Jesus stands with arms outstretched to welcome you.

I have met the real Jesus. And I know that the real Jesus is reaching out to you in the same way at this very moment. He is saying, "Come Unto Me." Perhaps you want to bury your head in shame because of the mistakes you have made in the past. He says, "Come Unto Me. Don't be ashamed. I already know all about that, and I still love you." Perhaps you would say to him, "I am facing a big problem right now. I don't know if I can manage." He reaches out his hands to you and he says, "Come Unto Me. We can work together on that problem."

This is the real Jesus – the one who wants to build you up, when life knocks you down – the one who can help you get up, when you want to give up. Come.

Come.
And you will learn …

The Secret of Unconquerable Strength.

In 1919, Lawrence of Arabia arrived at the Paris Peace Conference with a group of Arab Bedouins. As the desert nomads set foot in Paris, they could scarcely believe their eyes. There was water everywhere – the sweeping River Seine, the lavish fountains in every square, even hot and cold running water in their hotel rooms! Never had they imagined so much water!

Two months later, when it was time to return to the desert, everyone in the delegation agreed to meet at a certain time in the hotel lobby before making their way to the train station. But the appointed hour came and went. Lawrence waited, yet none of the Bedouins arrived. Puzzled, he decided to check on their whereabouts.

When Lawrence ventured up to their hotel rooms, he discovered the strangest sight – the Bedouins were tearing the faucets from the sinks and hiding them in their suitcases! You see, they believed that if they could just bring these marvelous French faucets back to the desert, they would have all the water they could possibly want.

Of course, they didn't understand that a faucet by itself is quite useless. It provides no water. The faucet must be connected to a water source, such as a river or reservoir, to provide water.

In the same way, human beings must be connected to the Source. If we desire all the good things that life offers, we must remain connected to the source of all those good things – Father God.

Perhaps you are at a place in your life right now where you feel like life has knocked you down. A particular situation has pulled the rug out from under you. A setback has knocked the wind out of you. You feel empty and weak. And you feel like you need strength greater than your own just to keep going.

Here, then, is the secret of unconquerable strength. It is simply this: You must be connected to the Source of strength.

To try to deal with these problems with your own power alone would be as foolish as trying to get water from a disconnected faucet. Without a connection to God, a human being cannot produce positive results. You will run dry. Your natural strength and creativity will evaporate. You'll get burned-out, bummed-out, and tapped-out.

Perhaps you would say to me, "Yes, Jeff, this is exactly how I feel right now." Then my prescription for you is this: *You need to optimize your connection to the Source.*

In fact, let me give you a three-step exercise program for building unconquerable strength. This system is simple, but fail-proof. I guarantee you this: If you work the system, the system will work for you. The first step is this …

Give God the first part of your day.

Before you even get out of bed each morning, say a simple but honest prayer. And here's the key: Make it a positive prayer – one that overflows with words of anticipation, enthusiasm, and hopefulness.

Pray something like this: "Good morning, Father! I'm excited about today! I'm sure You have some wonderful surprises lined up for me."

Then intentionally commit the entire day to God: "My day is completely open. Whatever it is that You're up to in this world, I want to be a part of it!"

Do you see how this simple prayer, spoken in your own words, before your feet even hit the ground and start running, sets the direction for the day? Do you see how you are already adjusting your attitude? You are moving your inner compass toward a positive pole.

Sadly, the majority of people do just the opposite. They live discouraged lives because they are perpetually programming themselves to operate on a negative wavelength. They begin the day thinking such things as:

"I'm dreading this day."

"I don't want to go to work today."

"Nothing good ever happens to me."

"I'll never be successful."

"I don't have what it takes."

"I'll never get out of this mess."

"I guess I just have bad luck."

My friend, don't pave the way for a bad day! Do you see what you have just done? You have prepared for defeat.

Thoughts are like seeds. By planting them in our mind, we allow them to take root in our subconscious. Soon they take on a life of their own; they grow and produce and multiply. If we begin the day with positive thoughts, our lives will constantly move in that direction. On the other hand, negative thoughts will constantly produce poor results.

So, what do you need to do? Program your mind! Don't allow pessimistic, critical, complaining thoughts to swamp you. Don't allow yourself to be defeated from the start by your own defeatist thinking. Instead, get up each day expecting great things, knowing God has great things in store for you.

This is exactly the opposite of what most people do. For most, their day begins with the unwelcome sound of their alarm clock. *Alarm* clock? Why, who in the world ever gave it such a frightful name? ("Oh, my! What is that sound? I'm *alarmed*!") Then they groan and drag themselves out of bed.

Instead, we should call it our "Opportunity Clock!" For each time it erupts, it signals the beginning of a new day of unimaginable opportunity. Remember, you are the Ultimate Optimist. All things are working together for good in your life. All events are designed for your benefit. All circumstances will ultimately work in your favor. For this reason, for you the start of a new day merely signals the start of one more day of improvement, advancement, and promotion.

To set your inner compass in this direction, pray something like this: "Father, I am excited about today! This is going to be a good day, because I know all things are working together for good and moving in my direction. Every day, in every way, things are getting better in my life. "

Does the day ahead offer little excitement? Pray: "I can't see what this day will hold. But I know that the little things are the big things. Therefore today is pregnant with potential. Perhaps a seemingly random conversation or unplanned encounter will open new doors for me – or even carry eternal ramifications. This could be the day that will be remembered forever in heaven."

Does the day promise little enjoyment? Pray: "Father, help me adjust my attitude. Maybe I'm not on vacation, or on a cruise ship, or traveling to an exotic location today. But I will be surrounded by people – and life is really all about love. Help me love and enjoy the people around me. Please bless me today. But, more than that, help me *be a blessing* to someone."

Now you have properly adjusted your attitude and set your mind moving in the right direction. Your mind is programmed for success. This is step one: Give God the first part of your day. Next ...

Give God the worst part of your day.

No one needs to remind you that life is difficult. Even though all things are working together for good in your life, some of the individual ingredients are quite distasteful. No one needs to tell you this; you are living it. Therefore the second step involves "getting through" what you're "going through." The key is to optimize your connection to the Source as you pass through those dark and difficult experiences.

As you enter into those stressful moments of the day, remind yourself that Jesus himself is with you. Yes, Jesus – the very same Jesus who burst out of the tomb vibrant and victorious – the very same Jesus who hugged the children, fed the hungry, and reached out his hand to touch the sick – that very same Jesus is with you at this very moment. He is with you as you go through those stressful moments, just as surely as he was with me, when we talked face to face on that hillside overlooking the night sea. He will be your source of unconquerable strength. Learn to tap into his strength by focusing your mind upon his presence.

What is it like to live in the constant awareness of the presence of Jesus? I recall hearing about a little girl who was quite gifted. One day, her Sunday School teacher gave paper and colored markers to all the children in class. The teacher instructed the children to draw a picture of Jesus.

The precocious youngster said, "I will draw a perfect portrait of Jesus."

The teacher said, "But, sweetheart, no one even knows for sure what he looked like."

The youngster said, "Oh, I do! And, when I'm done, you'll know, too."

Taking a bold red marker in hand, the little one set to work, busily filling her paper from top to bottom.

Moments later, she looked up and said, "Done."

She brought her artwork to the teacher.

What had she done? How did she create her "perfect portrait of Jesus?" She had simply copied the words of First

Corinthians 13, the famous "love chapter" of the Bible, onto her page. Remember the words of this beloved chapter? "Love is patient, love is kind…" it begins. But, as she wrote the words of Scripture, each time she came to the word "love" she changed it to the name "Jesus."

So the words on her paper now read like this: "Jesus is patient, Jesus is kind. Jesus is not filled with envy; he does not boast; he does not brag; he is never rude. Jesus is not selfish; he is not easily angered; he keeps no record of wrongs. Jesus is never happy when bad things happen, but he rejoices when good things happen. Jesus will always protect you. Jesus will always look for the best. And Jesus will never, ever give up on you."[50]

As the teacher examined her work, she did have to admit, it really was … the perfect portrait of Jesus.

This is what the real Jesus is like! If you were to meet Jesus face to face, travel beside him as I have, see him in all manner of circumstances – this is what you would see!

Knowing this, isn't it wonderful to know that this is the one with whom you will be spending your time? Isn't it wonderful to know that, when life knocks you down, this is the one who will be reaching out a hand to pick you up?

Focus on his nearness. Practice his presence. Picture him beside you – walking beside you as you go for a morning walk, seated beside you at the lunch counter in the diner, standing across the desk from you at work. Say nothing out loud – you don't need to make a show of this or a spectacle of yourself. But silently, in the quiet of your heart, pour out your feelings to him. Lay out your situation. As if you were in a business meeting, spread it all out before him.

You are now directly connecting to the Source and tapping into his power. You are not alone, as you face this current situation. And you do not battle this problem with your own resources alone. You are now drawing from his wisdom, his confidence, and his insight. And he has promised: "Never will I leave you; no, never will I forsake you … I am with you always, even to the end of the age."[51]

Now that you have spilled out your situation, remind him of the promises he and his Father have made to you. Mind you, he has not forgotten a single one of them. But it is important for *you* to recall them. It is critical that you firmly plant them in your mind. In this way, you are conditioning your mind toward the positive.

There are more than five-thousand promises which have been made to you in the pages of the Bible. If you don't have a Bible, get one – any modern day, easy-to-read one will do. If you do have one, open it. Begin reading about Jesus. You will meet him immediately in the opening pages of the New Testament. As you read, whenever you come to a promise, underline it. Rewrite it. Personalize it. Memorize it. Repeat it over and over. Let it become a readily available part of your thought-process and pattern of thinking. You are now reconditioning your mind from negative to positive. You are rewiring your synapses from an automatic, immediate, subconscious focus upon your problems to an automatic, immediate, subconscious focus upon your possibilities.

Uncertain what to even look for? Permit me to give you your first week's prescription. Take one a day, repeat as necessary.

Monday – "For we know that all things work together for good for those who love God …"[52]

Tuesday – "No good thing will He withhold from those whose walk is blameless."[53]

Wednesday – "For I can do all things through Christ who gives me strength!"[54]

Thursday – "Be strong and courageous! Do not be afraid; do not be discouraged, for the Lord your God will be with you wherever you go."[55]

Friday – "Call upon Me in the day of trouble; I will deliver you, and you will honor Me."[56]

Saturday – "Give all your worries and cares to God, for He cares about what happens to you."[57]

Sunday – "Do not be afraid, for I have redeemed you. I have called you by name; you are Mine. When you go through deep waters and great trouble, I will be with you! When you go through rivers of difficulty, you will not drown! .... For you are precious to Me. You are honored, and I love you."[58]

Commit each of those promises to memory. Write them out and place them on your mirror where you will see them first thing in the morning and last thing at night. Fasten each day's promise on your refrigerator door, your desk at work, or the steering wheel of your car. Fasten them where you will see them often … until they are at last securely fastened in your mind.

Maybe you're thinking, *I don't need promises or positive thinking. I don't need mental reconditioning. I need help – and I need it right now. I don't know what to do. I'm overwhelmed as I think about the future.*

I will tell you what you will do. You will do your best and trust God for the rest. You will put one foot in front of the other and keep going, taking it one step at a time. And you will make it through this day. Yes, you will! No matter how bad things look, you can make it through the next twenty-four hours, right? Think of it this way …

Think of your life as a mighty ocean liner, cutting across the waves. If the worst should happen, if that mighty ship should strike something and rip open its hull, what would the captain do? He would quickly press a few buttons high up on the bridge and, deep within the belly of the ship, great steel doors would begin to rumble and grind shut, sealing the ship into various water-tight compartments called "bulkheads." In this way, all leaks are contained and even a ship which is taking on water can remain afloat.

In the same way, when you are getting the worst of it, you must learn to shut off your life into "day-tight compartments." Shut out the past, with its failures and regrets. Seal off tomorrow, with its worries and uncertainties. And learn to live in this one, single, day-tight compartment called "today."

Now, can you make it through today? Of course you can! It's just one day. It will quickly pass. You don't need to set right all the mistakes of your past. No, not now you don't; not immediately; there will be plenty of time for that when things settle down. And you don't need to figure out all the potential problems of the future. No, the best way to prepare for the future is simply to do your best today. Instead, focus on making it through the next twenty-four hours. You can do that! With the presence of God, the promises of God, and the power of God – yes, you can!

My friend, I know that you feel like you're getting the worst of it. But what does an Ultimate Optimist like you or I do? *We make the best of it, even while getting the worst of it!* Don't make this worse than it needs to be. Cut this problem down to a manageable size. Seal it in a day-tight compartment, and I know you will not sink.

What must you do today? Just do your best and trust God for the rest. Give God the first part of your day. Give God the worst part of your day. And, finally ...

Give God the "thirst" part of your day.

For most of us, there is one particular area of our life with which we are dissatisfied. There is an ache. A hunger. A thirst.

We say things like:

"If only I could get my own home and get out of this apartment ..."

"If only I could meet the right person, someone to share my life with ..."

"If only I had a child – then I would feel fulfilled ..."

"If only I was making a little more money each month ..."

"If only this chronic pain and disability would go away ..."

What is *your* "if only?"

Almost everyone has one. It's the one thing in our life that causes us to say, "If only this area of my life was different, oh, then my life would be so much better!"

Whenever this "if only" rears its ugly head and pushes itself unwanted into your day, this is the "thirst" part of your day. It is when you feel that dull longing or acute hunger for something better than you are currently experiencing in your life. It is a thirst for something more.

"If God loves me," you protest, "why doesn't He give me what I thirst for?"

There is an eye-opening story in the Bible about a group of people who asked this very same question. In one of the most dramatic tales of the Bible, Moses leads the children of Israel to the Promised Land. Now, mind you, they witnessed all sorts of wonders along the way. The Red Sea opened before them; Pharaoh's army perished behind them; God's presence surrounded them. Still, the people of Israel soon felt the old familiar pangs of hunger gnawing at their bellies. They cried out and complained bitterly. Remarkably, at just the right moment, God sent them sweet frosty flakes of manna to feast upon.

Puzzled, some of the people came to Moses and said, "Why did God allow us to go hungry? After everything He did for us, we don't understand this!"

Moses told them, "God humbled you by allowing you to get hungry and then feeding you with manna. He did this to help you realize that real life comes from keeping your connection to God."[59]

Notice Moses said that God "allowed" them to get hungry. Why? He allowed them to get hungry so that they would recognize their need for Him, turn to Him, and depend on Him. He was showing them that to really experience life – real life, full life, life with a capital "L" – they needed to stay connected to the Source.

In the same way, God allows *you* to get hungry. He allows you to get thirsty. He allows dissatisfaction in your life. Why? He's trying to get your attention. He's trying to get you to turn to Him. *God wants you to reconnect to your Source.*

My friend, if you've got a problem, congratulations! God is trying to get your attention. If you're dissatisfied, congratulations! God is getting ready to do something in your life. The children of Israel never imagined that they would wake up one day and discover the ground covered with frosty flakes of manna. And you, my friend, can never imagine all that God has prepared for you!

You need to be like the young woman I read about recently. She was invited by a friend to attend church in her remote little village in Central Africa. From the moment the service began, the young visitor was completely engaged. There was genuine love among the members, as they greeted one another with hugs and smiles; there was palpable passion in the prayers, as they petitioned God to provide for their needs; there was heartfelt joy expressed in the music, with its throbbing African drumbeat. And when at last the old, white-haired preacher stood and spoke the sweet word of God, the young woman knew beyond a shadow of a doubt that she wanted to give her life to Jesus. But, to her dismay, she didn't know quite how. How was she to express her new found faith?

Well, as the service drew to a close, they prepared to gather the offering. Now, in their culture, they did not merely pass a plate solemnly from row to row. No, not at all! The offering was the very high point of the service – when the people of God got the opportunity to express their love, their joy, and their thanksgiving. As such, their custom was to form a line of people down the center of the church, sing boisterous music, and dance all the way to the front of the church, where they would personally deposit their offering in the big wicker basket before the altar.

As drums began to pound, as bodies began to sway, as joyful Christians began to sing and clap, the young woman joined the processional line and danced her way to the front of the church. When it came time for her to place her offering in the basket, what did she do?

The young woman placed herself in the basket.

She climbed in, gingerly placing one foot, then another, then finally her entire body in the offering basket. She, quite literally, gave her entire life to God.

There is no better offering.

Is there a thirst in your life? Are you hungry? Longing? Dissatisfied? Offer God your entire life. Like that young woman, give yourself to Him entirely, leaving nothing out. And like those desert wanderers of long ago, God might just surprise you with some sort of magnificent manna when you least expect it.

To see something different in your life, you must do something different in your life. What must you do to turn your life around? To find the strength to get through what you're going through? To pick yourself up after life has knocked you down?

Connect to the Source. Give God the first part of your day. Give God the worst part of your day. Give God the thirst part of your day. This is the secret of unconquerable strength.

And never for a moment forget …

The best is yet to come!

There was once a funeral for an old woman named Gertrude. Gertrude was very popular and beloved by all. As a result, on the morning of her funeral service, the funeral home was packed with people, all gathering to pay their final respects. There was, however, one thing which was quite strange. As her many friends filed slowly past Gertrude's open casket, they noticed something in her hand. Gertrude was clutching a fork!

Later, when the pastor stepped to the podium to address the gathering, he said, "I see that you're all wondering why Gertrude is being buried with a fork in her hand. Well, I can answer that. You see, Gertrude was active in our church for many years and she volunteered to help at all the church dinners. And always, when the dinner dishes were being cleared, she'd go from table to table to remind people to keep their forks because dessert was still coming. She'd always smile and say, 'Hold on to your fork. The best is yet to come!' My friends, Gertrude wanted to be buried with a fork in her hand to remind us that, even when you die, the best is yet to come!"

Gertrude was absolutely right. Even if you are facing the worst, even if you are staring down death itself, the best is yet to come! Here is what Jesus told us: "Do not be afraid. In my Father's house are many mansions. I will go there and prepare a place for you. Then I will come back and take you to be with me, so that we will always be together."[60]

Isn't it amazing to know that you have a mansion waiting for you? The one who knows you best, and loves you most, is the one who is getting everything ready for you. Then, at just the right moment, when your time on earth is complete and dark death is closing in, he will come and meet you. He will carry you in his strong and gentle arms to your home in heaven. The best is yet to come!

I can just hear someone say, "Well, I don't know. Are you sure there's a place in heaven for someone like me?"

Oh, yes, I am quite sure. I know Jesus and I take him at his word. He is getting everything ready for you, just as he said. One day you will be pleasantly surprised, just as a group of soldiers was one day pleasantly surprised.

A platoon of American soldiers, fighting in France during the Second World War, had an unsettling experience. One of their own, a popular young officer, was killed in fierce fighting earlier in the day. As the battlefield grew silent, the surviving soldiers crept from their foxholes and retrieved their fallen friend. They lifted him gently and carried his battered body back behind the lines, to an old medieval church that lay at the center of the little French village. Entering the ancient church graveyard, they began to prepare a place for their friend's burial.

Suddenly, a priest came bursting through the front doors of the church, looking quite alarmed. "You cannot bury your friend here," he told them firmly. "This graveyard is only for members of this church. We cannot allow outsiders to be laid to rest here. There is no room!"

So the soldiers decided to do the next best thing for their comrade in arms. They buried him just outside the graveyard fence.

The next morning the soldiers came back to say a final farewell before their platoon was shipped out. However, to their amazement, they could not find the grave! They carefully searched along the outside edge of the fence. They painstakingly traced their steps, back and forth, puzzled. But, search as they might, they could find no trace of the freshly dug soil.

As they were about to leave in bewilderment, the priest approached them. He told them that his heart had been troubled because of his refusal to allow their dead comrade to be buried in the church graveyard. So, early in the morning, while it was still dark, he had risen from his bed. And, with his own hands, he had moved the fence to include the body of the young American soldier who had died for France.

"Now there is room for him," offered the priest gently.

Will there be room for you in heaven? Jesus was sent into this world to tell you that God doesn't want anyone to be left outside in the cold. Early on Easter morning, while it was still dark, he rose from the dead. And, with his own bare, nail-pierced hands, he moved the fence. In spite of all the times you may have crossed the line morally, in spite of all the times you have lived your life out of bounds, there is a place for you in heaven.

"Now there is room for you," offers Jesus gently.

Do you remember what Jesus said to me on the morning of the resurrection? As that bright Easter morning dawned, he stepped from the darkness of the tomb and spoke words that still echo in my heart: "I am the resurrection and the life! Anyone who believes in me will live even if he dies!"[61] That was a promise meant for me – and for you.

Nine-year-old Hope Anderson knows how much that promise means. Hope never got a chance to say good-bye to her dad. She never got a chance to give him a final hug. Cancer put her dad in the hospital at the age of forty-two and little Hope was just too frightened to enter the Intensive Care Unit. Her dad never came home.

But Hope's pastor had an idea …

"Hope, can I talk to you?" he said after the funeral. "Sweetheart, my mom has cancer, too. She's going to heaven any day now. Would you like to talk to her and give her a message to pass along to your daddy?"

A phone call was placed to the bedside of the pastor's mom, Miriam Hatch, and a beautiful conversation followed. "Will you find my daddy and give him a message?" asked nine-year-old Hope. "Tell him I love him."

"I promise to give him a big hug from his little girl," said the dying woman. It was a touching moment between a little girl and an old woman.

Then, as the full fury of the cancer descended upon her in the days that followed, Miriam awaited only one final visitor, the Lord of Life Himself, who would free her and carry her home.

She departed for heaven at 3:04 a.m., her bedside surrounded by her children. But, just before she left this world, she wrote one final letter, a note to her new young friend. Here is what her letter said:

My dear Hope,

It pleased me so much that you called me today. You and I are two of Jesus' lambs, and he has promised to care for us. When he left, he said he would come again to take us to heaven to be with him there. Now, isn't that wonderful news?

Your daddy is already there. How happy he must be! I know I shall be going to that heavenly home, too. I shall meet your daddy, and I'll tell him about our special phone call.

Hope, let's keep telling others about Jesus and how much he loves us. That's what he wants us to do.

God will keep His arms around both of us. Someday, I will meet you in heaven. I'll expect a big smile from you!

Jesus' blessings!
Miriam Hatch

Death is not the end. The grave is not the end. The best is yet to come! Perhaps life has pulled the rug out from under you. Perhaps dark death is closing in, reaching for you with its cold grip. Do not give up hope. There is a Friend who met Miriam Hatch, stilled the storm of cancer, and carried her home. There is a Friend who found a way to bring comfort to nine-year-old Hope Anderson. And there is a Friend who calls to you today.

It is Jesus, the Lord of Life and Defeater of Death.

I can just hear someone say: "But, Jeff, I don't want to die. I'm not ready yet. I don't want to leave my loved ones."

You sound like a young mother I recently heard about. Her doctor said to her, "I have some bad news for you." She swallowed hard, as the doctor pulled the results of her latest round of tests from the file. "The cancer has spread."

"How long do I have?" she asked.

"Weeks – not months," he told her straight-out.

The words hit her like a slap in the face. Truly, in the most extreme sense, life was knocking her down. The wind was knocked out of her.

That afternoon, her pastor came to visit her in her hospital room. There, propped up in bed, the young wife and mother said, "Pastor, I remember in one of your sermons you said a thousand years is like a day to God and a day is like a thousand years. Is that true? Is a thousand years like a day in heaven?"

The pastor considered the question for a moment. "Yes, that is what the Bible says," he replied.

She said, "Good. Because I've been doing the math, and I figure if a thousand years is like a day, then forty years is like … an hour. I'll be leaving my husband and children soon. My husband may live another forty years. But that will be just like an hour for me in heaven. When he gets to heaven, I'll greet him and say, 'Where have you been for the past hour? Did you just go to the office or were you running errands? I've missed you.'"

Her expression momentarily darkened, and a tear splashed her cheek. She continued: "My children may live another seventy or eighty years. But that will be like two hours for me. When they get to heaven, I'll give them a hug and say, 'How was school today? Mommy misses you when you're gone for a couple of hours. I wonder how you're doing, because … because mommies don't like to be away from their children for long.'"

Two weeks later, she went to be with the Lord. The last thing she said to her husband was: "I love you. Take care of my children. I'll see you in an hour."

Here is what that young mom could now tell you. Here is what she has now experienced firsthand. She would say to you, "I will never forget the moment! Cancer was crushing me and the dark shadow of death was covering me. Death reached for me with its horrible, cold hands …

"But then Jesus stepped between me and death. He said, 'Hands off! She is mine!' At once, death crouched back into the corner fearfully. Then Jesus took me in his arms, hugged me close, and told me: 'It's okay. You're going to be alright. The best is yet to come!'

"Then he quite literally swept me off my feet! He lifted me from the hospital bed and carried me home. No, I will never forget the moment!"

And neither will you.

It will be the moment you will remember for all eternity.

It will be the story you will tell for all eternity.

It will be the long-awaited moment when you at last leave behind the "beforelife" so that you might finally begin to "Live."

What a moment that will be for you – the moment when, at long last, all your dreams will finally come true! You will walk through towering gates of glory, into the waiting embrace of those you love. A shout of welcome will arise in the air. Love will flow over you, like wave after wave of the soft, warm Caribbean Sea – love unlike anything you have ever known.

At that moment, your senses will be fully alive. Your mind will be sharp. Your pain will be over. Your weariness will be ended. As you take in the sweeping vista before you, you will experience a spectrum of sound and light and color that you never knew existed. You will see firsthand the glory of the City of Light and majesty of its King.

No, you cannot now comprehend what awaits you – no more than an infant in the womb can comprehend a world of light and color, a world of delicious meals and unfettered motion and unlimited space. No, now you cannot imagine it – but one day you will live it. You will see it. You will experience it.

Yes, for you, the best is yet to come!

The famous movie director Cecil B. DeMille once had a summer home on a little lake not far from my home in the rolling hills of Massachusetts. Let me share with you what he discovered one day on that lake …

One morning DeMille awoke early and decided to take his boat out on the lake. The sun was just pushing up over the pines, burning away the morning mist, sending sparkling diamonds of sunlight over the placid water. As DeMille reached for the oars, he noticed an ugly, greenish-brown beetle crawling up the side of his boat. He watched its slow, tired climb. Soon the beetle stopped moving altogether, the last of its strength expended. Lifeless, its exhausted body remained clinging to the spot where it died.

Reaching the center of the lake, DeMille took up a movie script and began reading as the boat drifted lazily over the lonely lake. Nearly two hours passed. As the sun rose higher and the day grew warmer, the dead insect's greenish-brown shell began to bake in the summer sun. It quickly grew dry and brittle. It cracked and withered.

Just then, looking up from his script, DeMille noticed something strange occurring. The dead, lifeless, withered beetle … was moving! It seemed to throb and rumble from within. A moment later, the brittle, brown, dead shell cracked completely open.

A tiny face appeared, thrusting outward, its large eyes wide and staring. Then, from the center of the cracked shell, a single silver translucent wing burst forth – then another. A newborn creature carefully pushed forth from the old, dead shell. Silently, it moved its gossamer wings up and down, slowly waving them first this way then that, drying them in the warmth of the sun.

Then, stretching its long, translucent wings to their full span, the newborn took off! Leaping from the old dead shell, it soared upward, its gossamer wings shining silver in the sunlight. De Mille watched in wonder, as the newborn darted back and forth over the surface of the lake.

DeMille had just witnessed the birth of a dragonfly.

He later told a friend of his experience. He said: "If God does that for an insect, which was created to crawl around in the mud … imagine what He does for a human being!"

Let me paraphrase the words of Cecil B. DeMille: "If God does that for an insect, which was created to crawl around in the mud … imagine what He will do for *you*!"

Yes, imagine.

Imagine indeed.

Key Discovery
The Best is Yet to Come!

Part Six

Entry 21
Back in the Beforelife

I can't see.

I am lost in darkness.

I am disoriented.

God, this cannot be happening to me again.

Am I in a tomb? *Again?*

I am lying down, stretched out, covered with linens. *Am I the corpse?* A heavy shroud presses down upon me, covering all but my face.

I am alone in the darkness of the tomb.

But, no, I hear crickets – not the silent vacuum of the sealed tomb. I hear breathing – next to me, soft, peaceful. I turn over, encumbered beneath the weight of the linens. And then I see a pale yellow light less than a foot away. It reads …

4:03.

A digital alarm clock. I'm back in my own bedroom. Back where I started. Was it a week ago? Or a second ago? Kathy is asleep beside me. It's just past four in the morning.

I'm back.

I pull back the covers, slip out of bed, and reach for my clothes. They're still there – thrown loosely at the foot of the bed where I left them when I undressed for bed a few hours ago. (Or was that days ago?) I feel my way through the darkened bedroom, reaching out for the doorknob that I can't see, but know by habit.

Going downstairs, I turn on all the lights. My dog, Rorie, looks up sleepily, barely stirring. He doesn't know I've been gone. He has no inclination of the millennia I've traveled since I last went up those stairs to the bedroom.

I walk around the house aimlessly. I want to look around. I want to believe I'm really here. I touch the cold smoothness of the granite counter top. I pet Rorie, running my hand over his soft, silky back. I want to tell him something silly, like "Jet sends her greetings," and the thought makes me smile.

I know I'll be up for awhile. There's no use trying to sleep. So many thoughts are swimming around in my head. Perhaps recording my experiences, just as they occurred to me, will help me make sense of all I've lived through. Perhaps spilling it out on paper will be cathartic. I sit down at the kitchen table, a fresh tablet of lined paper and a ballpoint pen in hand. I quickly record the words you now read, writing page after page in a scribbled longhand until my hand cramps and burns. I stand and pace about, clenching and unclenching my writing hand to get the blood flowing. I make a cup of coffee. And then I write more – much more.

When the sun peeks up above the tree line three hours later, I'm still at the kitchen table. The words flow easily, though I really can't imagine if they'll make much sense to anyone. I'm still too close to the events. I'm still too emotionally involved. I can describe what I saw and felt, but I'm not sure this rushing, tumbling flow of thought will be understandable to those who've not lived it. I'm sure it will sound fabricated – which is why I will not share my journal with others. How could I possibly get people to believe what has been happening to me? What would it take to convince someone?

I've witnessed how Jesus can perform miracles. Been there. Seen it with my own eyes. But, does he still do that for people? Even now in the Twenty-First Century?

Could he do it for me?

If only …

Later I hear the sounds of Kathy awaking. There's movement upstairs, followed by familiar footsteps coming down the stairs. Rorie jumps up from his spot at my feet and races to the foot of the stairs, tail wagging, eager to greet her. I understand! I have much the same feeling when I see her!

I pour Kathy a cup of coffee and take it to the table. I look at her, trying to read her eyes. The last time I looked into those eyes, they were reflecting the light of heaven. Now, she doesn't even acknowledge that anything out of the ordinary has occurred.

Does she remember any of it? Somewhere in her mind is there a trace of memory, a shadow, a glimmer, of an afternoon spent with me on the far side of eternity? Does she recall, somewhere in her subconscious, the soaring ramparts and gleaming gold of the City of Light?

Or, has that afternoon not even happened yet? Does it become a reality for Kathy decades from now, when, as an aged woman in a nursing home, she slips silently from this world into the next? I don't know. The simple explanations given by Jesus about time being like a yardstick, or a river, do not seem simple to me at all now.

"How did you sleep?" I inquire, looking for a clue.

"I was restless," she said. "I felt like I was tossing and turning all night."

There's an understatement! I think to myself. *More like tossing and tumbling ... through time.*

We quickly move through our morning routine and prepare for the day. The drive into the office takes less than ten minutes. I'm still moving through this day with a sense of unreality. After all I've experienced, I'm a man living in multiple worlds. I have a home and friends in the First Century. And I have a home, family, and friends in the Twenty-First. And I've spent an afternoon in still another home, a home that waits for me on the other side of this life, on the far side of eternity. The residue of each reality clings to my mind.

As I walk into my office, I notice the light on my phone is blinking, indicating that I have a message. I press the "Play" button and listen. It's an officer from the bank which holds the church mortgage. They want to telephone me later that afternoon, requesting a two o'clock teleconference, to "just get an update and ask a few questions."

My heart begins to race with anxiety. Lately, questions from the bank have not been questions easily answered. Not surprisingly, when loans are paid promptly, bank officers feel little need to question how decisions are being made. But, when loans fall behind, they naturally need to take action.

Now, with this telephone conference looming, my mind is forcibly drawn back into this reality. Like it or not, some difficult decisions will need to be made. And I'd better be prepared, no excuses.

The two o'clock conference does not go well. No, not at all.

At 2:03, the telephone beside my desk chirps. The caller I.D. identifies the name of the bank. As I pick up the receiver, I hear a slight echo on the line. This is not a good sign. This means they have me on speaker phone. This will not be a simple update with the loan officer I've been dealing with, on a nearly weekly basis, for the past two years. Instead, my words are being piped into the office of executives in Minneapolis whom I have never met.

"Jeff, there are some others in the room with me today," begins Meg, the loan officer who regularly handles our account. "My boss, Fred Johnson, who is the Vice President of Corporate Financing, is here with us. Steve Peterson, our Senior Loan Servicer is also joining us, as well as several others from accounting." A general murmur of greetings from the others reaches my ear. I respond warmly, as if their presence is a pleasant surprise.

There is a moment of uncomfortable silence, then Meg takes the lead. "Jeff, you've done a truly admirable job managing a very difficult situation. Really. We appreciate the personal sacrifices you've made. We know that you and your team have gone without a paycheck for weeks at a time, and we appreciate it. We know that you have done all you can do to control expenses, reduce staffing, and market aggressively. Few people we work with have your resolve …"

I'm waiting for the other shoe to drop. I have this dreadful feeling that Meg is softening me up for the death blow.

Another awkward pause. "Here's the thing, Jeff. We don't know how much more time we can give you. Please understand. We must do our due diligence and keep all our loans in good standing. In a very real way, our hands are tied. You must understand this situation from our point of view, Jeff. By law, we must report how this loan is being managed to state and federal regulators. They go through our files with a fine toothed comb to be sure that we're following all applicable regulations. On top of that, we have to report to our shareholders why this loan has gone south. They'll press us and question us about the return on their own investment."

Fred jumps in. "I guess what we're trying to say is, the time has come for some hard choices."

By "hard choices" I know what Fred means: foreclosure. I know that they believe they can break up the corporation and sell off the assets bit by bit to reclaim a fraction of their lost investment. The land is valuable – seventeen acres of prime multi-use commercial real estate. The building – just ten years old – would be prized office and retail space with plenty of frontage at the convergence of three state highways. The restaurant – poised on the edge of a main road – would be coveted by some.

"I understand," I mumble, my heart racing, darkness closing in.

"Your church has a four-million dollar loan with us. Interest on that loan is accruing faster than you can pay it. That is to say, the size of your debt is growing month by month. We see no sign of you turning this around."

"Meg ... you know me," I blurt out, pleadingly. "Fred, Steve ... Look, I've always been honest with you. If you give me the chance, I promise you I will do everything I can to pay off this loan completely – even if it takes the rest of my life. I've worked my entire life to build this ministry ..."

I can almost hear the air go out of the room. "Jeff, I'm sorry," says Meg. "We really don't have a choice."

I walk down the office corridor to Kathy's office. I walk in, shut the door behind me, and collapse in a chair.

"What is it?" she says, imploringly. "I can read your face like a book. Is it that bad?"

"Worse," I answer.

I begin to recount my telephone conference. I hate the look of fear in her eyes. It pains me. I want to protect her from this. But I can't keep it from her. Hypothetical discussions that we have had in the past year suddenly jump to the front burner.

"We could declare bankruptcy," I state, my voice emotionless, my heart sinking. "That would tie this whole thing up in the courts for another two years. Maybe that would provide enough time for the economy to pick up."

"But that could cost a fortune in legal costs," counters Kathy. "We don't have that kind of money. If we had a magic bundle of money sitting around somewhere we wouldn't be in this problem in the first place."

Silence just hangs in the air for a moment.

Kathy presses on. "I know you feel like God has called you to this ministry and you feel like it has been your life's work," Kathy offers. "And I'm in it with you. I am! But, if the worst happens, you know we could do this somewhere else. Maybe God is asking us to move on. And we might actually get a consistent paycheck!" she adds, trying to lighten the mood. "Maybe it's time to think about moving to another church and starting over ..."

"But the people in our church are like family to us," I counter. "We love them. We've shared so much for so many years. We can't just pack up our bags and leave them. It would feel like walking out on our family."

I know that Kathy agrees. She doesn't want to lose her church family. But she feels backed into a corner.

"We have *no income*. We'll lose *everything* – our home, our livelihood, even our church. What then?"

I'm grasping at straws, throwing out any idea we can grab hold of. "The church is more than just a building. If we lose the building, maybe we can rent an auditorium at the local high school for Sunday services. Maybe we could meet from house to house, like the first Christians did."

There is a long pause. "We could," counters Kathy, considering the possibility. "But we certainly wouldn't be the same church. We drew people by being a church with dynamic music, cutting-edge visuals, and captivating worship. We'd be starting over again. We couldn't duplicate our ministry in a rented school auditorium. And we couldn't offer the same programs. Think about all the children and families who think of this as their home! It's heartbreaking."

Another long, uncomfortable pause. Kathy's like Peter, action-oriented. I can see her thoughts suddenly shift direction. "I think we need to get out in front of this," she says, not sounding nearly as confident as her words. "We can't bury our heads in the sand and hope this will just get better. I say we put our house on the market immediately. If we wait too long and we can't make the payments on it, the bank will take it."

"Kath, you love that house. You designed it, found a beautiful piece of property to build it on, and put your heart into it."

"I'm not sure we have a choice."

"I know," I mumble.

Kathy looks hard into my eyes.

After a painful pause, she asks, "How long do we have?"

"They said they would give us to the end of the year. Today is November 10th. That means we have …"

Kathy finishes my thought: "Seven weeks."

I meet that night with the Church Council to brace them for what's looming in our future. There's plenty of discussion. There's plenty of anxiety. And there's plenty of prayer. There's just one thing we lack … a way out.

We burn through four of the seven weeks with no plan of action. My time is filled with holiday preparations. There's planning for Thanksgiving, Christmas activities, and Candlelight Services. There's preparation for holiday family gatherings. There's more than enough to keep my mind occupied and my calendar full. I'm like a little boy playing on a rocking horse: there's a lot of motion, but no progress.

I try not to think about what awaits me with the start of the new year. But, all along, in the back of my mind, every moment of every day, there is an inescapable dread. I should be The Ultimate Optimist. But instead, I give in to my fear.

This will be the last year I will celebrate Christmas with my family of faith.

This will be the last year my family will gather in our beautiful home.

This will be not just the end of a chapter …

This will be the closing of the book.

I think back … back to another time in my life … a time that felt like one book was closing and another opening. It was the day before I left for college. I was seventeen years old and about to leave home. Riding in the car with my mom, she suddenly turned to me and said, "I just want you to know that your father and I are very proud of you. And we're proud that you want to become a pastor."

Then she told me something that I had never known before, something I would never forget. Ever. As the familiar streets of my childhood passed by outside the car's window, she told me something deeply personal, something she had hidden in her heart for a long time …

"Jeff, when your father and I were first married, we wanted a family more than anything – more than anything! All our friends were having babies and starting families. My parents kept asking when we would give them grandchildren. It was the height of the baby-boom years! But I couldn't conceive. Month after month, we tried. Month after month, we were disappointed. A year came and went – then, two. Still, nothing happened. Eventually, *four years* had come and gone.

"Finally, I was desperate. I didn't know where to turn. Though I wasn't really religious, one night I called out to God and I tried bargaining with Him. I prayed: *If you give me a child, You can have him back when he grows up. You can make him a pastor.*

"I suppose you shouldn't bargain with God. I suppose you should just accept His will for your life. But here's the thing …The very next month, I discovered that I was pregnant!"

I looked over at my mother. I had never heard this story before! Where was she going with this?

She said, "Can you imagine how dumbstruck I was when, as a tiny boy, you suddenly announced to everyone that you were going to be a pastor when you grew up? Why, you weren't even in kindergarten yet! And, amazingly, your entire life you never wavered from this desire."

I was confused. The truth is, my parents never seemed to support my dream of becoming a pastor. Never. My parents were always firmly set against the idea. "You'll never make much money," they warned. "You'll work weekends and holidays for the rest of your life!" they complained. They even told me, only half joking, "If you have a church with three-hundred members, you'll have three-hundred people bossing you around! Do you really want that?"

As if reading my mind, my mom continued. "We never encouraged your dream. In fact, we always pointed out the downside of it all, because we didn't want you to feel like you had to become a pastor to please your parents. We figured that if God wanted you to be a pastor, then He'd find a way to place the desire in you. But, now that you're getting ready to leave home and begin your preparation to be a pastor, we just want you to know how proud of you we are. God called you to this before you were even born. He carefully shaped you for this and gave you every ability you would need to be a success. You were created on purpose, for His purpose."

My mom paused for a moment, then drew in a deep breath. "You are here today, Jeff, because God heard the prayers of a young woman who wanted to be a mom."

The memories of that day disappear as quickly as the mist on a Maine morning. As my mind resurfaces in the present, I think, *If all of that is true, God, how can You forget about me now?*

You custom-designed me for ministry. So why would You allow me to lose my ministry?

I am here in this world because one day God heard the voice of a young woman echoing in the throne room of heaven. Her words moved Him. That very day, something was set in motion.

My ministry began on that day.

Though I didn't make my entry into this world for another nine months, that was Chapter 1, Page 1. The story started with a prayer.

But now the last chapter is drawing to a close. The final page has been turned. On January 1, the book will end. That's how I feel.

My ministry began with a prayer.

To be honest, now, I don't feel like I've got a prayer …

On Thursday, December 1, I receive an e-mail asking if I would be available to take a telephone call later that day. "If it would fit into your schedule," requests the e-mail, "I would like to call your office this afternoon at 3:30."

Curious, I e-mail a reply, indicating that I would be available.

At exactly 3:30, my office phone chirps. The caller I.D. simply reads, "Undisclosed Caller."

"Good afternoon," I announce, sweeping the receiver up to my ear. "This is Jeff, can I help you?"

"Jeff, yes, hello. This is …"

On the other end of the line is a man I have never met before.

He is not from our region of the country.

He has never once attended our church.

He has never once donated a dime to our church.

I wouldn't be able to pick him out of a crowd if my life depended upon it.

I *have* spoken to him on the phone a number of times over the past four or five years. And I have answered a fair number of detailed questions about our ministry. He is now calling from his car phone.

"Jeff," he begins, his voice gentle and quiet. "I want you to know that I believe strongly in your leadership. I believe in your vision. I want your ministry to be successful."

He wastes no time on small talk, but gets right to the point. "Therefore, I would like to write you a check …"

Suddenly my breath catches in my throat and my heart begins to pound.

"… a check for $500,000."

I make no response. I'm not sure I heard this right. Somehow the reality of this conversation is not sinking in.

"I want you to use this check to pay off the interest your church owes the bank."

My mind cannot process such a swift change in fortunes. There must be a catch. I'm waiting for the other shoe to drop.

"Would that be acceptable?" he asks politely.

I stammer, "I… I … think that would be acceptable."

He continues: "Jeff, you're still struggling under the weight of that same old debt. Nothing has changed in terms of your current cash flow. I know that. I'm just catching you up to where you would have been if the recession never pulled the rug out from under you …. So I want to do more. I don't want to just help with the past; I want to do something to change the future. So I'd like to help you bring your mortgage down to a more manageable size."

I swallow and say, "Okay."

"In addition to the $500,000 I'm donating immediately, I'm prepared to offer you an additional $1,000,000 over the next three years."

With great control and sophistication, I say, "Gulp." Or, at least, this is what I think I say. I may have emitted some sort of guttural sound.

He quickly adds, "Let me clarify. I will provide Christ Lutheran Church with $1,000,000 in *Matching Funds* over the next three years. This is not just a hand-out. Your people have to do their part, too. If your church members rise to the challenge, I will match everything they give, dollar for dollar. Is that an offer your people could get behind?"

I don't answer.

I don't answer … because I'm unable to form words. I'm unable to express a single coherent thought.

I am … awe-struck.

My pulse is pounding in my ears and I try to breathe in and out, slowly and evenly. I'm still holding the phone, but my eyes are closed … and I picture Jesus smiling. I imagine the look on his face at this very moment. I'm sure he is grinning from ear to ear, thinking, *Didn't I tell you to just trust me?*

I burst into Kathy's office. "What?" she asks. "What happened? Why are you looking at me like that?" She takes a long look at me. "Are you crying?"

"I think I am!" I exclaim. My eyes are pooling. I'm overcome.

I spill the whole story out to her. I run through a list of scribbled notes that I took while I was on the phone. I jotted down bullet points as we spoke, not wanting to forget a single detail.

By the time I spit out just a sentence or two, Kathy's eyes are filling up also.

What a sight we must be to anyone who passes by our office door and glances inside! Our lives have just changed – forever – in the space of a single ten-minute phone call. Like a convict on death row, just hours from execution, we have been handed a last-minute pardon. I reach for a Kleenex and hand it to Kathy to daub her eyes. Then I reach for her and take her tightly in my arms.

Before the day is over, I personally call each member of our Church Council and share the news of our phenomenal turn of events. These are the easiest telephone calls I have ever made! Each board member is … what? What words can describe the feeling of a crushing weight being lifted? Joyful? Exultant? Relieved?

"Blown away." Yes, that's it. They are "blown away."

With extreme difficulty, I share the news with no one else. With such a dramatic turn of events, I want to be sure that our message is communicated in a way that is clear, consistent, and accurate. (I know how quickly rumors can take off, spreading like a wild fire, whether accurate or not.) I also know, from hard experience, that it is best to remain cautious until the arrangements are finally complete and every detail worked out. In this case, I decide to tell no one about our windfall until the check is cashed and the funds clear. (I can only imagine the horrible disappointment and the loss of credibility that would follow if I make a grand announcement only to be forced to later admit that the deal fell through.)

A fifteen page legal agreement is faxed to me the next morning, laying out the details of our agreement. The exact nature and timing of the dispersal of matching funds, the anonymity of the donor, and the required mortgage account routing numbers are specified. Agreements and signatures are needed between the donor, the bank, and the church.

By the following Wednesday, December 7, I receive word from our bank that the funds have cleared.

With this one deposit, three years of a faltering economy have been erased.

Instantly.

Wednesday, December 7 – the day the check cleared.

Before the day ends, I send out word to our entire congregation, via our e-mail "Constant Contact" program, that I will make a major announcement on Sunday morning. "Please don't be absent this week," I write to my family of faith. "I will be announcing something that will be of critical importance to our church."

As Sunday approaches, curiosity is reaching a fever pitch. "Is the bank taking our building? Are we facing foreclosure?" some ask, alarmed. "Is Pastor Jeff leaving us?" ask others.

On Sunday morning, there is anticipation filling the church as people file into their seats. The air is thick with tension. When I stand and walk to the podium, a hush falls over the room. I begin speaking ...

"You are about to hear the story of a modern day miracle ... a miracle that takes place in a little town in Massachusetts ... in a little church – a church that had a little bit of faith ... and a great big God."

Now silence hangs in the air. Eyes dart back and forth to one another.

"Friends, all of *you* are going to be the cast of characters in this miracle story ..."

Then, taking a deep breath, I let the news drop ... and it hits them like an atom bomb.

As the realization of our church's magnificent miracle fully dawns upon them, the entire congregation erupts in jubilation. From one end of the room to the other, people rise in a standing ovation – not an ovation for their pastor, not an ovation for their anonymous benefactor, not even an ovation for their amazing windfall. It is a spontaneous standing ovation in honor of God!

That week I deliver the same message to all five worship services. The standing ovation is repeated at each.

On Tuesday, December 13, I receive a telephone call from a local reporter. I learn that our tiny community newspaper, *The Westfield Evening News*, is planning a story on the generous gift we received from an anonymous benefactor. They fact-check a few items and promise to be in touch if they need more information.

The following day, when I arrive at my office there's a photographer waiting at the front entrance of the church to capture a picture of me entering. He asks if he can take a picture of me standing in front of the church. Then he asks for a "head shot" and directs me to turn my face this way and that.

Laughing, I ask him why he's suddenly so interested in me.

"Haven't you heard?" he says, with great animation. "The Associated Press picked up your story. They're calling it *'The Christmas Miracle.'* Your church has just gone nationwide!"

When I walk into my office, my telephone is ringing – and it doesn't stop ringing for the next forty eight hours. I am deluged with calls from reporters and requests for TV appearances. The story of our "Christmas Miracle" is carried by all the major television networks. ABC, NBC, CBS, CNN, and FOX all love a heartwarming human interest story to help their viewers get into the spirit of the holiday season. They run the story repeatedly. The New England News Network blankets our region with the rags to riches tale of our church; the World News Network takes it global.

By week's end, we are written about from one end of the country to the other. Our story is carried by newspapers as far flung as the Houston Chronicle, the Indiana Daily Journal, the Boston Globe, and the Hartford Courant. A google search on our church brings up a listing of news articles that is nearly thirty pages long!

My parents see me on ABC Channel 10 out of Albany, New York, while an old college professor from whom I have not heard a word in decades contacts me to tell me he saw me on the morning news in Miami, Florida. A foreign exchange student who is studying for a semester in Europe calls her mom to say that she saw Pastor Jeff on TV in Spain!

Oh, how Jesus must be smiling!

Surely this is now objective, verifiable proof that God has been doing something miraculous in my life. My goodness, how could my friend Jesus have arranged anything more dramatic! Though few would believe the words of my journal, words that spoke of tripping through time and falling through millennia, who could possibly deny this latest chapter? Why, anyone, anywhere, could just google "Christ Lutheran Church, Southwick" and read the entire story from a dozen different TV stations and newspapers!

By the time our church gathers again for worship the following Sunday, the story of our amazing gift is being called "The Christmas Miracle heard round the world."

As I stand before my family of faith, all I can do is shake my head. I say humbly, "This week the story of our Christmas miracle caught on worldwide. It's a great human interest story. It's heartwarming. But, my friends …" Then I pause to rivet their attention upon what I will say next.

My voice thunders: "That story is still being written!"

My voice fills every inch of the room. "Men and women, this story is just getting started. And all of you are the cast of characters." Again I pause, so there will be no mistaking my challenge. "Now – with the whole world watching – we must make the most of this amazing opportunity!"

The challenge is clear.

I look from face to face.

I wonder what the next chapter of this story will hold.

Christmas Eve falls on a Saturday – a cold, clear night less than one week after I issued that challenge.

This year we will host six Christmas Eve Candlelight Services – and they will all be full. Eager men and women pack the church, still riding on a wave of emotion. Animated children sit beside parents and grandparents, and they are excited about more than just Santa. The music is breathtaking. The candlelight is captivating. The auditorium is decorated with over a dozen glittering Christmas trees, including one that towers thirty feet in the air. But the focal point is clear: A life-sized manger scene is set up at the front of the church, causing children to crane their necks to catch a glimpse of the Baby Jesus.

Near the end of the worship celebration, it's time for the offering. But on this night, rather than pass a plate among the people, we will do something special. We will invite people to walk to the front of the church and personally place their gift before the manger. We will invite them to become a part of our Christmas Miracle. More than that, we will invite people to offer their very life to that Child of Bethlehem.

As I invite people to come forward, men and women begin rising all over the room. A line of people, stretching from one end of the room to the other, begins to make its way quietly to the foot of the manger.

I watch from the front row. I watch as people I love bow their heads in silent prayer and place their gift before the Christ Child. I watch as children hold the hands of their parents and quietly place hand-drawn birthday cards for Jesus at the foot of the manger. Some bring elaborate pieces of art, covered with stickers and glitter, as their gift. Others have drawn simple stick figures or written a few words. I watch a group of teenagers gather, arm in arm, around the manger. They pray, hand in hand. Then they place a check in the manger. Some have given their entire paycheck for the week. Some have given their entire savings. They have pooled their money in order to give a single large gift. They, too, have become part of the Christmas miracle.

Still the line continues flowing slowly forward. I watch one man – a tough, old, craggily-faced construction worker – sink to his knees before the manger. Soon, entire families fall to their knees before the crèche of the Christ Child, then rise with cheeks tear-streaked and hearts full.

By night's end, a great mountain of generosity has risen up. Offering envelopes, crumpled bills, neatly written checks, and loose change – together with dozens of drawings, toys, and even Christmas cookies – add to the Christmas miracle.

Most important, a mountain of lives has been offered. White-haired grandparents and bright-eyed middle schoolers, hard-working parents and idealistic teens – all have given their hearts on this quiet, candlelit night.

Truly *this* is the Christmas Miracle.

The decisions they have made, the gifts they have given, the love they have offered, will echo into eternity. This candlelit Christmas Eve night will be remembered in heaven long after the world forgets …

The story of "the Christmas Miracle heard round the world."

"I'm going to be a pastor when I grow up!"
I announce when I'm five years old.

Here I am leading worship in my parent's basement.
I made the altar from a cardboard box
and painted the initial *J* on it for *Jesus*.

Jet and Rorie:
"Hey, Rorie, Jet sends her greetings!"

Christ Lutheran Church, Southwick, Massachusetts:
We wondered, "Does God still do miracles,
or did things like that only happen in Bible times?"

The fifteen page legal document has just arrived.
Little did I know that this day would soon be known as
"The Christmas Miracle heard round the world!"

The announcement of our "Christmas Miracle"
brought standing ovations at all five services!

After the Associated Press picked up our story,
our "Christmas Miracle" made headlines around the world!

Kathy and I

Entry 22
One Year Later

It has been one year since I was crucified.

Donations keep coming to support our "Christmas miracle." We're paying down our mortgage at the remarkable rate of $20,000 per month.

Apparently, I've stopped tripping through time. I have not "fallen" again. My life has settled into normal patterns and routines. Now, with the passage of time, I can make some sense of what I've experienced. I have some perspective.

What has it all taught me?

Hmmm… where to begin …

I have learned to be The Ultimate Optimist. Yes, I've learned to look up, when I feel like giving up. I've learned how to pick myself up, when life knocks me down. And I've discovered a "Source" of unconquerable strength.

And you have learned this, too! Yes, if you've gone with me on this journey, traveling through these pages with me, you've discovered this, too.

And, yes, after months of worrying about losing our home, the "Christmas Miracle" turned things around. But here's the funny thing. Knowing that Kathy and I have a home waiting for us in the far reaches of eternity now means infinitely more to me than knowing we have a home waiting for us at the end of the work day in Massachusetts. Ironic, isn't it? I feared the loss of the modest three-bedroom house that Kathy designed.   Yet I will one day inherit the custom-built home Jesus himself designed.

I know. Looking back on it, it seems like I'd have to be completely dense not to make the connection sooner. I mean, not too subtle! But, that's Jesus for you. Usually he has to make the point as big as a billboard before I get it. *Are you smiling, Jesus?*

If you're looking for a billboard of your own, let this be it: Jesus has a home waiting for you, too. Spectacular. Custom-built. Perfect for you. It's been described as a "mansion."[62] And, best of all, it's a gift. The one who knows you best and loves you most has everything already prepared.

Now, as I open this journal one last time, let me encapsulate what you and I have discovered on this whole, long, astonishing journey.

Principles of the Ultimate Optimist
How to Pick Yourself Up... When Life Knocks You Down

Part 1

Jesus is more powerful than the storm. I remember being in that little wooden fishing boat, far from land, as the furious storm clouds descended upon us. I remember the ferocious wind, the wild raging waves, and the exploding lightning. But I also remember Jesus stretching forth his hand and quieting that storm. The simple fact is, we will all sail through some storms in life. Perhaps you're caught in one now. Dark clouds hang over your finances, your marriage, or your health. You feel like you are about to go under. But the important thing to remember is: No matter how big your storm is, Jesus is bigger.

You need to get in the boat. The one critical decision you must make in the midst of your storm is this: Will you try to go it alone, or will you ride it out with one who has the power to still the storm? Determine that you will go through this storm with Jesus. This is the key. This one decision will change the entire trajectory of every event that follows.

You're going to be alright. These are the words you need to hear: "You're going to be alright. You're going to get through this. Even if the worst happens, you're going to be okay." How do I know? I know, because you are now traveling through this storm with the one who has the power to still the storm.

Key Discovery
Get in the boat.

Part 2

Life is about love. Do you feel like your life isn't working? Perhaps you've been looking for happiness in all the wrong places: in popularity, possessions, pleasure, power, or prestige. But these are all things which are short-lived. Each will eventually be lost. And you were created to be a lover, not a loser! Lasting happiness is found when we align with our primary purpose in life: giving love and being loved. Jairus learned this lesson the hard way. He nearly lost his little girl. Now he would tell you exactly what I'm telling you: Life is about love.

Life is empty without love. Remember the young woman who had been sick for twelve years? I do. I remember her pale, drawn face. I remember her sunken eyes and sallow cheeks. And I remember what she said to us: "The worst part is that for twelve years – twelve lonely years – I have been shunned. I am alone." She was telling us what our heart already knows: Life is empty without love. We were wired from the very start to give and receive love. Since this was the very reason for which we were created, a life without love will be an empty and joyless one indeed.

It's not too late for love. God Himself is ready to pour love into your life. There should be no shortage! Perhaps you've been hurt in the past. You feel dead on the inside. You feel like God must be disappointed with you. But you are still God's much loved child. He has never given up on you. His love is unwavering. Perhaps you're thinking, *I don't deserve that. I don't feel worthy of that kind of love.* But His love for you is unconditional. He wants to love you like His own cherished child. Here is what we discovered: Just as deeply and desperately as Jairus loved his little girl ... Father God loves you.

Key Discovery
Let God love you.

Part 3

Your problem is not a problem. Jesus is aware of your situation. And the good news is: Your problem is not a problem to Jesus. He has not been taken by surprise. He already has the solution. Remember that golden afternoon by the sea, when Jesus fed thousands with a few loaves and fish? If Jesus could so easily handle that situation, he can handle your situation.

The little things are the big things. Jesus took time to play with the children. Even though his day was filled with many demands, he hugged them and held them and blessed them. That's because Jesus understood this one simple fact: The little things in life really are the big things. You may be going through a difficult time right now. You may think you are unable to make a difference. You may feel weak and ineffective. But the world turns on small hinges. One small, seemingly inconsequential, event can have enormous, even eternal, ramifications. Indeed, a monarch flapping its wings in Malibu might cause a monsoon in Malaysia! In the same way, a moment spent with a child, a smile given to a friend, or a chance encounter in the grocery store aisle may be the catalyst which will change the course of history! Even if you feel like life has knocked you down, this very day could be the day that changes everything. This day might be the day that will be remembered for eternity.

It's a bounce back world. Remember the little boy who heard his own echo? Remember the farmer who faithfully scattered his seed across the barren field? Remember Jesus explaining the Law of the Harvest? Here is the lesson: What you give is what you get. Your actions, words, and gifts will bounce back to you like an echo. What you send out in life inevitably, invariably, inescapably returns to you. More than that, it returns to you in multiplied form! Therefore, you yourself have the power to determine the level of blessing and bounty in your life.

Key Discovery
It's a bounce back world.

Part 4

God has a plan – and it is good. Do you remember the moment? On a lonely, windswept mountain in Galilee, I caught a glimpse of glory. I saw Jesus transformed before my very eyes. I listened as he spoke to Moses and Elijah about a plan that had been set into motion before the dawn of time. And you and I play a part in this plan! You have a distinct role to play. More than that, this divine plan is designed to work to your advantage. All things are working together for good in your life. All events are being coordinated for your benefit. Each day's developments are moving in your direction. Therefore you can be The Ultimate Optimist!

The road is rough – but don't give up. Be an optimist, but also a realist. What should you do when you are facing difficult challenges? Do your best and trust God for the rest. Do not be stopped by "obstacle illusions" – for you plus God are bigger than any obstacle. Yes, certainly each day will hold its share of challenges. But, like the woman who discovered the twenty dollar bill hidden inside her Bible, God has already placed within you everything you will need.

Your situation is difficult – but not impossible. Do you remember what Peter blurted out? Jesus glowed with glory as he talked with Moses and Elijah on the mountaintop. Peter asked, "Do you want me to build some shelters for you?" He was remembering a lifetime of *"sukkot"* celebrations. This is what you should remember, too. When life feels empty or hopeless, remember the lesson of the *"sukkot."* God will provide for your needs. He has not forgotten you. Trust Him totally.

Key Discovery
Become the Ultimate Optimist.

Part 5

The True Fall Guy. Jesus intentionally "took the fall" for you and me. He died for us. In this one act, he solved our biggest problem. Now, he calls to us personally, longing to be a part of our lives. Like the famous statue of Jesus in the Copenhagen Cathedral, Jesus is reaching out to us saying, "Come Unto Me."

The Secret of Unconquerable Strength. Lawrence of Arabia had to explain to his Bedouin friends that a water faucet must be connected to a source of water in order to produce the desired results. In the same way, a human being must be connected to God to produce the desired results. He is the Source of all that is positive in this universe. How do we maximize this connection? Here is a practical prescription: Give God the first part of your day, the worst part of your day, and the thirst part of your day. Like the young African woman who climbed into the offering basket, offer your entire life to God. This is the secret of unconquerable strength.

The Best is Yet to Come! Remember Gertrude? She reminded everyone, "Hold on to your fork, for the best is yet to come!" Gertrude was absolutely right. Even if we face death itself, the best is yet to come! We can be assured of this because Jesus has prepared a spot for us in heaven. Like the French priest who personally moved the graveyard fence to make room for a fallen soldier, Jesus personally removed the barriers to make sure there was room for you and me in heaven. Knowing this one dynamic fact entirely changes our perspective on life. Now we see that our current problems, however pressing and painful, are only temporary. This is merely the "beforelife." Real "Life" awaits us. And it will be better than we can imagine! As Cecil B. DeMille put it: "If God does that for an insect, which was created to crawl around in the mud ... imagine what He does for a human being!" Yes, imagine what He will do for *you*!

Key Discovery
The best is yet to come!

I turn the page. I put down my pen. I don't know what to write next. The page is entirely blank. I stare at it.

Maybe this is what your life looks like right now. It's a blank page. It's a story yet to be written.

But know this: Long ago, a barren young woman asked God for a child – and *I* came along! Before I was ever conceived in my mother's womb, I was conceived in the mind of God. I was custom-designed. I was given everything I would need to fulfill the plans God had for me. I was made on purpose, for a purpose.

And so are you.

You were conceived in the mind of God. You were custom-built. You were fully-loaded. You were carefully designed. You now possess every talent, every ability, and every gift you need to be successful in this world. You now possess every good break, every grand blessing, and every great opportunity that you will need to fulfill the purpose for which God created you.[63]

You were made on purpose, for a purpose.

Maybe you feel like life has knocked you down. Maybe circumstances have pulled the rug out from under you. Maybe you can't see any answers to your problems. But keep this in mind: A year ago, I could not conceive of any possible way out of my problems. As I scanned the horizon, failure and foreclosure were the only images on my radar screen. I could not imagine a "Christmas miracle heard round the world." And, at this moment, you cannot imagine what God has lined up for *you*.

I only know this …

There are pages yet to be written about you – yes, entire chapters!

And it will be good.

Entry 23
Final Entry

It's been three years since I was crucified.

I'm jacked. Pumped. Amped. Stoked. Soaring. (What's the right word to describe this heart-quickening, fully-alive, raring-to-go feeling?)

It's Easter Sunday morning – the biggest Sunday of the year! The church is packed, standing room only. The third of five back-to-back services has already started. I stand behind the door, waiting for the burst of applause that will mark the end of the opening music and my signal to go on.

I hear the final crescendo building, flip the on-switch of the wireless microphone that is strapped to me, and listen for my cue. I'm already smiling from ear to ear. All joy and energy and excitement, I will charge through that door and out to that podium like a lion being uncaged.

There it is – my cue!

I place my hand on the door, swing it open, and step into …

Darkness.

A sudden gust of wind whips my hair back. A chill runs through me. I smell the brackish air of the sea. Above me, the sky is swollen with stars. Before me, a few lonely fishing boats labor slowly over the surface of the sea. I see men pulling in their nets, hand over hand, sweat glistening in the light of their torches.

I am in Galilee.

I'm back.

The last time I was here they crucified me.

I step carefully through the thick brush that lines the dunes, feeling my way through the darkness, eyes adjusting. Reaching the coarse white sand of the beach, my walking becomes less labored. I look about, uncertain. *Which way should I head?* I walk to the water's edge and begin hiking toward the lights of an outlying village.

In the distance, a man sits warming himself before a charcoal fire, his back turned to me. I make out his stooped silhouette in the darkness. He is about a hundred yards ahead. I draw closer, wary, my steps quiet in the sand.

I hesitate, deciding whether to move any closer or simply turn around before I'm spotted. I'm a big man. I'm in good shape. I can hold my own. But it's never wise to creep up on a stranger, in a strange place.

Just then, he lifts his head, turns slightly and listens.

A shiver runs through me. This could be a trap. I have no idea how many men might be hiding in the brush above the dunes. I have no idea if he is armed.

The stranger stands, stretches, and begins to turn in my direction. There is something familiar about his silhouette.

All at once, the fireworks explode within me. *It's Jesus!* No longer hesitant, I begin running toward him.

When I reach him, I throw my arms around him, nearly knocking him over. You've seen soldiers returning from war. You've seen the crying wives, the thrilled children, racing forward just to feel their arms around their returning hero. I am like this. I crash into Jesus, laughing and crying at the same time.

"I can't believe it!" I exclaim, practically shouting in his ear. "It's so good to see you!" I'm holding him at arms length, but I'm not letting go. I'm staring at him, absorbing every line on his face, every fleck of color in his eyes. It's been three years – three years since a bloody cross, a dark tomb, and a bright dawn.

He just beams back at me.

"Why didn't you tell me? That night on the hillside, overlooking the sea – why didn't you tell me?"

He knows I'm talking about the Christmas Miracle. I want to know why he let me go through all that angst and anxiety. "You could have just told me!"

"But I did," Jesus replies, smiling easily. "I said, 'Just trust me.' Didn't I say that? What more needed to be said?"

Yeah, I get it. Point well taken.

"But I … I …" Now I'm stuttering, tongue tied, my thoughts racing faster than my mouth can form a sentence. I pause, unable to find words which will carry the depth of my emotions. This man has done so much for me! I look into Jesus' eyes, holding his gaze without saying anything. Silence hangs in the air.

Then I just shake my head. "Thank you." I search for something else. But in the end, I just repeat myself: "Thank you."

He holds my gaze a second longer. Then, a smile slowly rises to his lips, brightening like the sunrise. Without saying a word, he acknowledges my gratitude with the smallest nod of his head.

"Come on, Jeff," he says. "Let's have a seat by the fire and shake off the cold. I've got some fish on the coals. Fresh bread, too. The sun will be up soon and we can have some breakfast."

I notice the sky has changed from black to gray. Birds are beginning to flit about us, chirping and singing cheerfully. The gulls are busy, poking about at the water's edge, searching for breakfast. Soon, the golden Galilean sun will push over the horizon, gilding the sea.

As I sit beside the warmth of the glowing charcoal, I marvel at the love this man has for me – this friend, this Lord. I am filled with a sense of wonder.

"Jesus, can I ask you something?"

He looks up. He is carefully turning each fish in order to broil both sides equally. He pauses. "Always. You can talk to me about anything."

"Why me?" I ask, barely above a whisper. "I mean, there are a thousand other churches that need help. But, out of all the churches in the world, my church was given an out-of-the-blue Christmas Miracle? And there are a million other people who need special attention, who've gotten in over their heads, who've fallen down, or whatever. But, out of all the people in the world, you decided to personally take time to mentor *me* one-on-one. Why? Why me?"

"I told you already, Jeff. You're special to me. I see something in you."

Wow. Holy Cow. What have I done to deserve this? I am suddenly filled with a deep, holy sense of awe – and wonder beyond words. Then, suddenly, at last I see it. Suddenly I see that his heightened level of love for me says more about him than it does me. It's not so much that I'm a remarkable man ... it's that he has a remarkable capacity for love.

Jesus looks up. "Look, there they are," he says, breaking my train of thought. He points to a commercial fishing boat passing by about a hundred yards out. "I figured you'd want to see them one more time. Have a chance to catch up." He adds: "Things are changing quickly for them, Jeff. It's been a little more than a week since they saw me dead and buried. Now, well ... now they're still just trying to adjust to the new reality of Easter and of not seeing me around all the time. Trying to wrap their minds around what the whole thing means. You've got a unique perspective on it, Jeff – a two-thousand year perspective. That's why I arranged this little breakfast."

Jesus rises and walks over to the water's edge. The sky is brightening, but the sun has not yet pushed over the rim of the horizon. The fishing crew is making their last run of the night, dragging their net through the charcoal-black water.

"Friends," he calls out to them in loud voice, "you didn't catch anything tonight?"

"Not a thing!" they shout back, their disappointment carrying across the waves.

I can see little more than shadows and silhouettes, but I recognize the voice. It is Peter. He is out with a crew, dragging the waters. I think I can make out John, and Andrew, too, and some of the others. Naturally, Peter would want to get to work again, rather than just sitting around, left with nothing but his thoughts. He is a man of action. He likes activity – and, besides, a good catch will provide some income for the days ahead.

I can't tell if the men recognize who it is that is calling out to them. Are they aware that it is Jesus? They've only seen him twice since his resurrection. They aren't expecting him.[64]

He shouts a suggestion to them: "Throw out your net on the other side of the boat and you'll find some fish."

The crew has been out all night, fishing by the light of torches. The light usually draws the fish. Yet, tonight, they've caught nothing. Simply shifting their net to the other side of the boat should make absolutely no difference. Moreover, the fish are unlikely to be drawn to them now that the sky is growing light. Yet, remarkably, the tired men do as they're told, with no argument.

They cast their net out, a large circular net weighted with lead plugs. It splashes quietly as it hits the surface, then sinks from sight. The boat continues to slide silently over the black sea. Then, suddenly, there is a fury of churning waves, white-water, and silver bellies. The men are taken entirely by surprise, and nearly pulled overboard! Soon, the entire crew gathers around the bulging net, heaving together, exerting all their strength. But, even so, the men are unable to haul the net into the boat because of the large number of fish trapped within.

Suddenly Peter realizes who it is that is standing upon the shore. He's seen this type of thing happen only once before.

Three years earlier, along this same beach. It was the morning when Jesus first invited him to retire from the fishing business and join his little band of disciples. At once, awareness dawns upon Peter.

Jesus and I watch as Peter does something which is ... well, so *Peter*. He has been working all night – hard, dirty work – so he is stripped down, wearing only his loin cloth and short-sleeved tunic. Peter immediately abandons the net and reaches for his clothes. He impulsively throws on his robe. He carefully arranges it and fastens it in place. And, now, properly dressed ... he leaps into the water! Yes, so *Peter*.

Peter swims wildly back to shore to see Jesus, splashing and sputtering and shouting all the way. Watching him, Jesus turns to me, grinning from ear to ear. "You just can't help but love him – am I right? How can you not love a guy like that?" he says.

Before I can answer, Jesus takes a long look at Peter and says, "He is special to me. I see something in him."

It is the same thing Jesus has always said about me.

But I feel no jealousy. I feel it takes nothing away from me. For now I see the truth. I should have seen it long before. It should have been quite clear to me as I watched him play with the children, attend to Jairus, listen to the stories of the people who came to him in the crowds.

This is how he feels about each of us.

This is how he feels about *you*.

Let this thought reverberate from one end of your heart to the other ...

You are special to him. He sees something in you.

Peter plows toward us, splashing noisily through the water, scaring away any fish that might still be in the area. As soon as his feet touch the sandy bottom, he begins running, climbing up out of the water onto the shore. Clomping out onto the beach, water streams from his drenched robe and drips from his sopping hair and beard. His wide, dark eyes are locked on Jesus, exuberant and animated. Then suddenly he sees me.

For an instant, he does a double take, blinking back his shock. Then Peter races across the beach on squishing, slapping sandals and throws his burly arms around me. He lifts me right off the ground, then drops me back down and pounds my back with his fists. I'm completely soaked from his hug, but I don't care. It's just so good to see him.

"I ... I thought you were dead!" he exclaims.

Words tumble out of his mouth awkwardly. "They told me..." He begins a sentence, then drops it. Suddenly, Peter doesn't know what to say. He thinks he has to say something, anything. The last time he saw me, after all, was the night I was arrested. This big guy, who's all heart, hangs his head, looking at the ground.

"I ran away."

It's a confession, spoken barely above a whisper. As if I didn't know.

Silence hangs heavy between us. His discomfort, his remorse, is excruciatingly evident.

"I heard horrible things ... about what they did to you ... to Jesus ...."

His voice catches in his throat. Finally he says simply, "I wasn't there for you." The words barely come out. I hardly hear them over the sound of the crashing waves.

For me, it's in the past. I can't hold a thing against him. I nod my head and gently reply: "What else could you have done? I would have done the same thing. Anyone would have."

Peter can't think of any words that sound right. So he just shrugs.

This time, it's me who can't find the words. Some things are too deep for words. So I just take a step forward … and give my friend a hug.

Peter grins that big sheepish grin.

I step back, look at him, and roll my eyes. "You always go swimming dressed like that?" I say, pretending to mock him. Now he knows things are back to normal.

"You always disappear when there's work to do?" he shoots back.

We both laugh and start walking toward the edge of the water, waiting for the others to make land.

With some effort, the crew brings the boat to shore, towing the swollen net full of fish in its wake. Now the others spot me. They begin shouting to me, joyful and incredulous to see me alive! I stand on the water's edge, waiting.

When they reach the beach, they drag the prow of the old wooden boat onto the sand, muscling it up out of the water. Jesus and Peter immediately climb aboard to help drag the net ashore. I wait, take hold, and pull from the beach as the net reaches the sand. Once the catch is safely on land, we open the net and begin the process of sorting and counting. The work goes quickly. We're happy just to be together. We're happy to be with Jesus.

"Bring some of the fish you've just caught," Jesus suggests. "Come and have breakfast."

We follow Jesus back to the warmth of the charcoal fire. The sand is soft and cool beneath us, as we sit in a tight circle around the fire. Jesus serves us, going from one to another. As we eat, we talk, the words spilling out. We talk about what we've been through. We talk about what the future will hold. They tell me how it felt to be there on that first Easter evening, when Jesus suddenly stood among them, shocking them and sending their emotions spinning.

They, of course, have absolutely no conception of where all of this will lead. I try to open their eyes, urging them not to place any limits on what this little team will accomplish in the months ahead. They look at me blankly. To them, I'm just another Galilean peasant, like a hundred others they've known. They have no idea.

Jesus tells them they will carry the message of his resurrection to the very "ends of the earth." I can't even begin to tell them what this means – I could speak to them of distant continents and cultures and centuries, of teaming millions and martyrs and a movement that will rock eternity! But it's beyond them. All of it. Beyond anything they can imagine.

In truth, they're now concerned only with the immediate. They cannot see the big picture. From their perspective, the small picture entirely blocks their view. So Jesus addresses the situation which is most on their minds at this moment. It concerns Peter. There is unsettled business with Peter – and, for the men, it's hard to see beyond it.

You see, the night we were arrested, Peter caved. He quit. He folded. And the men can't get over it. So complete was his collapse, he cowered even before a little servant girl. Not once, but three times, Peter swore to high heaven that he never even met Jesus!

To this group, sitting close around this fire, this is not old news; this is recent history. There is only one thought in everyone's mind. It hovers just below the surface, unspoken. After quitting, is Peter even welcome in this group anymore?

Jesus charges in, tackling the situation head-on. Yes, Jesus can be direct with people. Even blunt. I have seen it.

"Peter," he says.

Peter's head jerks up. He opens his mouth to speak, but says nothing.

An uncomfortable silence settles over the entire group. *Here we go.*

"Peter, do you love me?" Jesus asks.

The words burst out of Peter. "Yes, Lord!" The words come immediately, as if he's been waiting for this. "Yes, you know that I love you!"

Jesus neither smiles nor blinks. He levels his gaze upon Peter. His words are solemn. "Feed my lambs."

The others around the circle look one to another. *What is that supposed to mean?*

But still Jesus does not stop staring at Peter. "Peter, look at me." There can be an intensity to Jesus, a raw energy. This is one of those times. Peter is locked in his energy field. "Peter, do you love me?"

The same words. A second time.

Carefully, deliberately, because he wants Jesus to know that he means it, Peter answers, "Yes, Lord, you know that I love you."

Still solemn, still serious, Jesus speaks in a tone barely above a whisper. "Be a shepherd to my sheep."

Tears fill Peter's eyes.

And now the others are quite sure of what Jesus is doing. He is reinstating Peter. He is telling Peter that he is not only still a part of this circle, but that he will be in charge of caring for others as well, like a shepherd cares for sheep.

Still, even then it isn't over. Jesus rises and makes his way directly to Peter's side. He kneels before Peter. He places a hand on his shoulder and peers deep into his eyes. "Peter, do you love me?"

A great silence hangs in the air. Someone moves, but no one says a word.

As Peter looks into the eyes of Jesus, he sees such kindness that he cannot help but cry all the more. "Lord, you know everything. You know that I love you."

"Then feed my sheep."

Three times Peter denied knowing Jesus. Three times Peter has reaffirmed his love. Three times Jesus has reconfirmed Peter's calling.

At that precise moment, the edge of the sun peers over the horizon. It gold plates the water and gilds the clouds. A new day has dawned.

I feel the warmth of the rising sun upon my face.

The final words I hear Jesus speak to Peter that day are simple ones …

"Follow me."

I suppose this is, in truth, the invitation he issues to each of us.

"Follow me."[65]

After a moment of awkward silence, Peter clears his throat and looks about the circle sheepishly. "Well, look at all of you guys with your silly grins. What a sorry bunch I'm stuck with," Peter jokes roughly.

The guys grin all the more.

"Well, listen, it's time to get today's catch to the market," says Peter, rising and stretching his weary muscles. "This is going to be a good day for us."

We all stand. Jesus says, "Just a minute, Jeff. I have something else I need you to do. You others go on ahead."

My attention perks up. I make my way over to Jesus, as the rest turn toward the boat. I'm eager to help. I'm eager for a special assignment. *He sees something special in me.*

"Jeff, I need you to go back."

I am suddenly deflated. "Back? Back home? But when will I see you again?"

"When you need me most."

"But … but, when will that be?"

"Just trust me."

There it is again. I think this is a lesson I should know.

Jesus smiles, and when he smiles it's as if the morning sun rises within me.

"At just the right moment, when you need a friend the most, I will be there," he promises. "Don't be worried. Don't be afraid. One day – one day soon – I will take you to be with me and we will be together forever." He looks deeply, knowingly, into my eyes. "You will love the home I have prepared for you."[66]

I smile, inside and out.

I am not afraid.

I am special to him.

I turn and feel the Galilean sun, warm upon my face. Just then, a strange disequilibrium … a momentary lightness …

I feel the bright stage lights of the church warming my face. I am mid-stride to the podium.

It is Easter Sunday. And I am …

The fall guy.

The thief on the cross.

The angel at the tomb.

The Ultimate Optimist.

The recipient of "the Christmas miracle heard round the world."

I am Jeff, an ordinary man.

As I step to the podium, I think of Jesus, as he was a moment ago – standing in the early morning light beside the Sea of Galilee.

I pump my fist in the air, the universal sign of victory. "He is risen!" I proclaim as never before.

The entire church thunders back: "He is risen indeed!"

Indeed.

Author's Note

"I swear only this: that every word I tell you is true."

With these words from Part One, my story gripped the initial readers of this book and created a shock wave. Did all of this actually happen? Is Jeff really claiming to "slip between centuries?" Is God granting him remarkable visions ... or, on the other hand, is he just delusional?

Let me offer some clarification.

The events described in this book which occur in First Century Galilee are factual. They are recorded for us in the timeless pages of Scripture. They are verified by volumes of historical research, archeological findings, and extra-Biblical sources.

The events that depict my own life story are also factual. Each of the details – from my mother's heartfelt prayer for a child, to a dog named Jet, to a "Christmas miracle heard round the world" – are true. Remarkable. Yet true.

Moreover, the lessons outlined in this book are true. The Principles of the Ultimate Optimist are taught in the Bible and verified by experience.

However, I do not "fall" through the centuries. This is a literary device which I have employed to enable readers to feel as though they are truly experiencing Biblical events firsthand. As a Bible teacher at heart, I wanted the Bible to "come alive" for readers and grip them with the intensity felt by the first Christians.

Yet, in a deeper sense, we can all slip through the centuries. Whenever we open the Bible and scan its timeless pages, we are drawn into the world of Jesus. Whenever we open our heart in prayer, we enter the presence of the Eternal God.

In this way, we are all, in truth ..."The Fall Guy."

Acknowledgements

I owe a deep debt of gratitude to the gifted preachers and teachers who have gone before me. This book is filled with stories, anecdotes, and ideas which are by no means original to me. In many cases, they are classic illustrations which have passed from preacher to preacher. In most cases, I no longer recall where they originated.

I was fortunate to grow up in the church, always seated at the foot of a powerful pulpit. Moreover, I have been a teacher, preacher, and public speaker my entire life. As a pastor and a follower of Christ, I have listened to countless sermons and presentations over the years and I have been deeply influenced by many individuals. Some were classic communicators such as Robert Schuller, Joel Osteen, Rick Warren, Max Lucado, or Norman Vincent Peale. Others were little known to the public, yet deeply influential to me – such as my wife, my mother, my friends. I wish to express my gratitude to all who have touched my life or contributed to this book. My intention in writing this book is simply to pass on the blessings, and to God be the glory.

I also wish to thank the people of Christ Lutheran Church. You invited me to be your pastor when I was a very young man – immature, inexperienced, and untried. For more than a quarter of a century, you have stuck with me, through a few dark valleys and through more than our share of bright dawns. For this I thank you. Being your pastor and friend has been the honor of a lifetime.

I owe a particular debt of gratitude to the loyal, loving staff who has shared this long journey with me. You have become more than colleagues and friends. You have become family. Thank you for all you do each week to make our ministry exceptional.

Special recognition belongs to Kathy Elias, who always proves to be unwavering in friendship and unlimited in talent, and Margo Rosati, who serves with excellence and efficiency.

In particular, I must offer credit to Kathy King and Kathy Elias for their invaluable help in preparing this project. My wife Kathy not only believed in and supported this effort from the start, she was its first reader, editor, and creative advisor. Her mark upon it is indelible. Kathy Elias also served as a gifted editor and graphic designer. As is so often the case in our ministry, we three worked as a team and the end result was stronger because of it.

Finally, to those who taught me whatever I know about love – my parents, my children, and my wife.

To my parents – Ron and Marlene. There has never been a day of my life when I have not felt loved. There will never be a day when you will not be loved.

To my children – Jordan, Shaanan, Zachary, Ethan, Amy, and Jessica. I say to you what Jesus says to me: "I love you. You are special to me. I see something special in you."

Most of all, to you, Kathy. You make every day a "wow" day. I can't wait to carry you across the threshold of the home that Jesus has prepared for us in that City of Light!

Soli Deo Gloria.
Jeff

Discussion Guide

Part One

Read About It

The disciples were caught in a ferocious storm – and it was terrifying! The storm was immediately followed by the dramatic face to face encounter with Legion. Read the original eyewitness account of this series of events in Mark 4:35 through 5:20.

Talk About It

1. We all go through "storms" in life. What is the biggest storm you have ever experienced in your life? What storm are you in right now?

2. Would you describe yourself as riding in the boat with Jesus, watching from the shore, or in over your head?

3. What specific step would you need to take to truly "get in the boat" with Jesus and travel through the storm with him?

4. In the midst of the furious storm, Jesus was sound asleep in the back of the boat. (See Mark 4:38.) How do you react when Jesus seems to be "asleep" in your life? How does this story encourage you in those situations?

5. The story of the storm ends with these words: "They were terrified and asked each other, 'Who is this? Even the wind

and the waves obey him!'" (Mark 4:41) How did their fear *during* the storm differ from their fear *after* the storm?

6. After Jesus healed Legion, he said, "Go home to your family and tell them how much the Lord has done for you!" (See Mark 5:19.) What could you tell your family about what God has done for you?

Part Two

Read About It

Meet Jairus and his little girl in Mark 5:21-43.

Talk About It

1. When life knocks us down, we often withdraw into ourselves, pushing others away. What is your support system like?

2. Do you feel "surrounded by love?" What specific steps can you take this week to connect with others and increase your loving support system?

3. How does a parent feel when his or her child is going through a difficulty, illness, or crisis? (Explain by relating a personal experience.) How do you think God feels when you are going through such things?

4. Of the people mentioned in this story, who are you most like? In what way?

5. What does it cost Jesus to be involved in a relationship with you? What does it cost you to be involved in a relationship with Jesus? What does it cost you to be involved in a relationship with others?

6. What people have the greatest healing influence in your life? In whose life are you a healer?

Part Three

Read About It

It was a perfect spring day. Slowly read the description of what happened on that day as it is recorded in Mark 6:30-44. Pause after each paragraph to focus on what your senses would be taking in at that very moment. (For example, the warmth of the Mediterranean sun, the hunger in your belly, the smell of fresh bread.)

Talk About It

1. What does the phrase "the little things are the big things" mean? Give an example. How does understanding this simple phrase help you cope when you are feeling discouraged?

2. "It's a bounce back world." Based on your actions this week, what should you expect to see returning to you in multiplied form?

3. "Give, and it will be given to you," said Jesus. "And, with the measure you use, it will be measured back to you." (See Luke 6:38) Do you need to change what you are giving and sending out in this world? Do you need to change the measure you are using to send it? What one change do you most need to make right now?

4. Jesus said, "You give them something to eat." (See Mark 6:37.) How do you think the disciples felt when they heard this? How do you feel when you are faced with an overwhelming sense of need?

5. "How many loaves do you have?" pressed Jesus. (See Mark 6:38.) Why do you think Jesus asked this question? What was he asking his disciples to do?

6. What's the lesson in the story of Jesus feeding the multitude? In light of your current situation, what does this story say to you?

Part Four

Read About It

What a sight it must have been! History calls it "the Transfiguration" – the day Jesus permitted his disciples to catch a glimpse of his glory. We simply call it … amazing! Read Mark 9:2-8. What one word best describes this experience? Now read Mark 9:14-32. In contrast, what word might best describe this experience?

Talk About It

1. Why do you think Jesus took time for this long trip into the mountains just a few weeks before his death? Why was it important to Jesus to permit his closest friends to temporarily glimpse his glory? Why was it important to his disciples?

2. How often in your life are spiritual highs followed by problems, challenges, and temptations? Why isn't the Christian life more of a plateau experience, rather than highs and lows? Where do you learn more – highs or lows?

3. What does it mean to become "The Ultimate Optimist?" Explain in your own words.

4. Why does God seldom do something for us that we can do for ourselves?

5. Explain the significance of the *"Sukkot."* How was this annual celebration an expression of our trust in God's provision?

6. Describe the growing tension and pressure that Jeff is describing in his life at this point in the story. What pressure are you under in your life right now? How can the members of this group help and support you?

Part Five

Read About It

They were the two most pivotal events in human history: the crucifixion of Jesus ... and his resurrection on Easter Sunday. Imagine being an eye-witness, living through the emotional turmoil of that historic weekend! To capture a sense of the extreme highs and lows of those dramatic hours, read Luke 23:32-43 and Mark 16:1-8.

Talk About It

1. The flogging and crucifixion were graphic. What detail do you think would be the worst for you to endure? Thank Jesus for what he endured for your sake.

2. At what point in your life did you come to realize that Jesus died for you? (As a child, years ago, just recently, or I'm not sure that I have?)

3. What impresses you most about Jesus in this story? If Jesus was not the Son of God, how would you feel about him?

4. How is God a source of strength in your life? How is God *the* Source? What specific actions are necessary on your part to stay connected to the Source?

5. While being cheered in heaven, Jesus held up Jeff's hand to share the glory with him. In what way has Jesus done all the work, but shared the glory with *you*?

6. Imagine the moment you arrive in heaven. What are you most looking forward to seeing and experiencing?

Part Six

Read About It

The final story recorded in the New Testament Gospels is, likewise, the final story recorded in this book. Read about the early morning meeting that took place on the beach in John 21:1-25.

Talk About It

1. Why do you think Jesus repeated the same question three times to Peter? How is Peter supposed to demonstrate his love and loyalty to Jesus?

2. Out of all the principles taught in this book, which is the most important? Why? Which is the most practical and immediately applicable to your current situation? What specific action step do you need to take based on your answer?

3. How has reading this book changed your views of Jesus? What aspect of his personality most struck you?

4. Have you invited Jesus into your life? ("Get in the boat.") If so, what are you specifically doing to maintain and deepen your relationship? ("Stay connected to the Source.")

5. Ephesians 2:10 tells us that we are God's "workmanship." The original Greek word used in the Bible can also be translated "work of art" or "masterpiece." It further reveals that we were each individually designed to accomplish things which "God prepared in advance for us to do." In other words, each of us was created on purpose, for a purpose. (Jeff shared the true story of his mother's prayer to illustrate this.) What are the implications for your life if God created you with a specific purpose in mind?

6. Jeff describes the Christmas miracle as "a story still being written." How is this true in each of our lives? What do you think the next chapter will look like for you?

Notes

[1] See Mark 4:35-41. The Gospel of Mark is used throughout this story as our primary source because of its vivid, action-filled descriptions. Furthermore, this Gospel is generally believed to be based upon the eye-witness memories of Peter, a central character in this narrative.

[2] See Mark 5:1-20.

[3] See Mark 5:21-34.

[4] See Mark 5:35-43.

[5] See Matthew 22:34-40.

[6] See Mark 6:14-29.

[7] See Mark 6:30-32.

[8] See Mark 6:33-34.

[9] See Mark 10:13-16.

[10] See Mark 6:35-44.

[11] For more on the little known plot to kidnap Jesus, see John 6:15.

[12] For more on the use of the original Aramaic word *Abba*, see Mark 14:36, Romans 8:15, and Galatians 4:6. This term is expressive of the close, intimate relationship that exists between a parent and child.

---

[13] For a similar conversation, see John 21:15-17.

[14] See Romans 8:28.

[15] See John 3:16.

[16] See Luke 6:38.

[17] When Moses conferred with Jesus about his approaching death, he used the term "exodus." Jesus' saving death was no doubt connected in Moses' mind to God's saving of His people out of Egypt during Moses' own lifetime. Though often translated simply as "departure," the New Testament literally uses the Greek word *ex-o-dus*. See Luke 9:31.

[18] See Mark 9:2-8.

[19] See Mark 9:9-10.

[20] See Mark 9:14-27.

[21] Though Jesus was originally from the remote northern village of Nazareth (Matthew 4:12-17), Capernaum was used as his base of operations throughout his years of public ministry. Therefore, Capernaum was generally considered to be his home. (See Matthew 4:13 and Mark 2:1.) Capernaum was strategically located on the northern shore of the Sea of Galilee and thus provided convenient transportation throughout the entire region by boat.

[22] See Matthew 17:24-27.

[23] See Isaiah 55:8-9.

[24] See Romans 8:28.

[25] See Psalm 23:6.

[26] See Psalm 23:1-6 and Romans 8:28-39.

[27] See Mark 14:32-52.

[28] See Mark 14:53-15:20

[29] Though better known by the name "Calvary" (Latin, *Calvaria*), the original word used in the New Testament to describe the place of Jesus' crucifixion was literally "Cranium" (Greek, *Kra-ni-oum*), meaning "Skull." (See Matthew 27:33, Mark 15:22, Luke 23:33, and John 19:17.)

[30] It is impossible to capture the full power of the triumphant announcement made by Jesus moments before he died. The statement is typically translated, "It is finished." However, in the original text, it is a powerful and concise one-word proclamation. Employing the common Greek business term *te-tel'-es-tai,* the word can mean "Paid in full" or simply "Done." Moreover, the original Greek text emphasizes that when Jesus spoke from the cross, he did not whimper, he "roared." (See Matthew 27:46, Matthew 27:50, Mark 15:37, and Luke 23:46 where the Greek word is translated "cried out with a loud voice.") Jesus died as a victor and he completed what he came to do.

[31] See Matthew 27:32-56, Mark 15:21-37, Luke 23:26-49, and John 19:16-30. The *crurifragium* is described in John 19:31-37.

[32] See Revelation 21:1-22:6.

[33] See Luke 23:43.

[34] See John 14:1-3.

[35] See Matthew 27:62-66 and 28:11-15.

[36] See Luke 24:1-12.

[37] See John 11:25-26.

[38] See John 14:19.

[39] See Mark 16:1-8.

[40] In a similar way, Moses absorbed the glory of God into his own body. After being in God's presence, the face of Moses was so dazzling white that "the people of Israel could no more look right at him than stare into the sun" (2 Corinthians 3:7 MSG).

[41] Much has been made of the "young man dressed in white" in Mark's account of the resurrection. Matthew tells of one angel being present on Easter morning (Matthew 28:2), while Luke describes two (Luke 24:4). Yet Mark speaks only of a "young man dressed in white" (Mark 16:5). Critics have long contended that these discrepancies represent obvious errors and inconsistencies within the Biblical accounts. Yet these differences in description should not be considered troubling. Frequently only the spokesman is specifically noted in Biblical narratives, while an accompanying individual is not mentioned. Furthermore, words and postures often change in the course of events (seated, John 20:12; standing, Luke 24:4). Therefore, these variations are not necessarily contradictory. They are merely evidence of independent eye-witness accounts of the same event. While I assign myself a role in these events for dramatic purposes, I find no contradictions or puzzling mysteries within the Biblical accounts.

[42] See 1 Peter 2:24.

[43] See Romans 3:10-12 and Isaiah 53:6.

[44] See 1 Peter 3:18.

[45] See Romans 5:6-8.

[46] See John 3:16.

[47] See Romans 6:23.

[48] See Isaiah 49:15.

[49] See Matthew 11:28.

[50] See 1 Corinthians 13: 4-7.

[51] See Hebrews 13:5 and Matthew 28:20.

[52] See Romans 8:28.

[53] See Psalm 84:11.

[54] See Philippians 4:13.

[55] See Joshua 1:9.

[56] See Psalm 50:15.

[57] See 1 Peter 5:7.

[58] See Isaiah 43:1-4.

[59] See Deuteronomy 8:3.

[60] See John 14:1-3.

[61] See John 11:25.

[62] The traditional King James Version of John 14:2 describes our home in heaven as a "mansion."

[63] See Ephesians 2:10.

[64] This early morning appearance of Jesus on the shore of the Sea of Galilee is now his third post-resurrection appearance to Peter (John 21:14), though there had been appearances to other individuals. Jesus first appeared to Peter in Jerusalem sometime during the day on Easter Sunday (Luke 24:34). Later, he appeared to Peter again that same evening when the disciples were gathered together in the upper room (Mark 16:14, Luke 24:36-43, and John 20:19-25). Next, he appeared one week later, as the disciples were meeting again in the upper room in Jerusalem (John 20:26-31). This explains why, in my telling of the story, Peter seems more shocked to see me alive than he does Jesus. As a result, he immediately runs to greet me and express his astonishment.

[65] See John 21:1-19.

[66] See John 14:1-3.